Sky Blue, Grass Green

Written and illustrated by
Susan Kropa

GOOD APPLE, INC.
BOX 299
CARTHAGE, IL 62321-0299

ISBN No. 0-86653-355-9

Printing No. 987654

GOOD APPLE, INC.
BOX 299
CARTHAGE, IL 62321-0299

ACKNOWLEDGEMENT

I wish to acknowledge the editors of *Arts and Activities* and *School Arts* magazines for their encouragement and support over the years.

TABLE OF CONTENTS

Clay

INTRODUCTION

Sky Blue, Grass Green is the second book in the series that began with *Faces, Legs, and Belly Buttons.* It is aimed at primary grade children (six, seven, eight-year-olds). If you want a recipe book with simple instructions and predictable results, this is not it. If, however, you value art experiences and consider art an important part of the overall curriculum, read on.

Are you still with me? Good. The term *art* as used here means more than just a finished product, although that is part of it. Art is also an attitude, an approach to problem solving, a means of expression which draws (no pun intended) on mental resources that are untapped in other subject areas. Studies of the brain have shown that our educational system teaches largely to the left hemisphere, that is to the logical, rational side of the mind.* The right hemisphere, which houses intuitive, creative abilities, has to fend for itself and is often stifled. Art triggers the creative spark.

Young children learn through all of their senses. They experience their surroundings by watching, sniffing, touching, tasting, and listening. Before reading and language arts begin to dominate their thinking, children are at their creative best. The trick is to help them preserve the playful, imaginative part of their minds as they grow older.

The first part of the book discusses the artistic developmental level of primary grade children. It will give you an idea of the kinds of things you can expect in the artwork of first, second, and third graders. There is a brief section on motivation, followed by ideas for projects.

My philosophy in planning art activities takes the middle path between laissez-faire and dictatorship. If done properly, guiding, showing, and

*For more information, read *Drawing on the Right Side of the Brain* by Betty Edwards.

demonstrating, all have their place. Children, like everyone else, get better results when required to work within given limitations. You can imagine the panic you would feel if someone handed you a set of watercolors and said, "Paint **what**ever you want, **how**ever you want." On the other hand, to take away **all** choices reduces art to pointless busywork. As in any other school subject, there are many ways to approach and build on a single concept in art. Variety in presentation or medium keeps children interested, while subtle repetition of key concepts helps them grow. While some of the activities are original, most are traditional, but with a new twist. You should feel free to alter them to suit your needs and personality. Activities which might fit into several categories are listed in the table of contents according to the main or most important concept being taught. Grade level is suggested at the beginning of each lesson. Many activities can be adapted up or down.

Whether you are parent, classroom teacher, or art teacher, you will find this book useful. More than that, you will get a feel for teaching art the way it should be taught.

GROWTH AND DEVELOPMENT

Before you become an "art teacher" in a classroom or the kitchen with your own children, you should know what to expect from your young artists. Art educator Viktor Lowenfeld described the stages children typically go through in their artistic development. His book, *Creative and Mental Growth,* is the basis for most art education methods courses. Unfortunately, because his writings are so specialized, parents and teachers who could greatly benefit from his findings have never heard of them. The following pages will give you an overview of Lowenfeld's theory.

SCHEMA

According to Lowenfeld, children in the primary grades are in the "schematic stage."* Don't let the technical name bother you. A "schema" is a symbol for something real. Around the age of five or six a child will begin to use the same symbols over and over again. It isn't as important to know how he arrived at his symbol system as it is to recognize that each child's is as personal as his handwriting.

*As in other areas of education, there is a wide range of ability in art. In a classroom or family, some will be at the top end of the spectrum and others nearer the bottom. Obviously, children don't proceed through these stages on the same timetable.

HUMAN SCHEMA

By the end of kindergarten, most children will be drawing people in more detail. They may now include eyebrows, hair, hands, feet, fingers, neck. Hands, feet, and faces are good places to look for a child's symbol system. Below are some examples of what you might find.

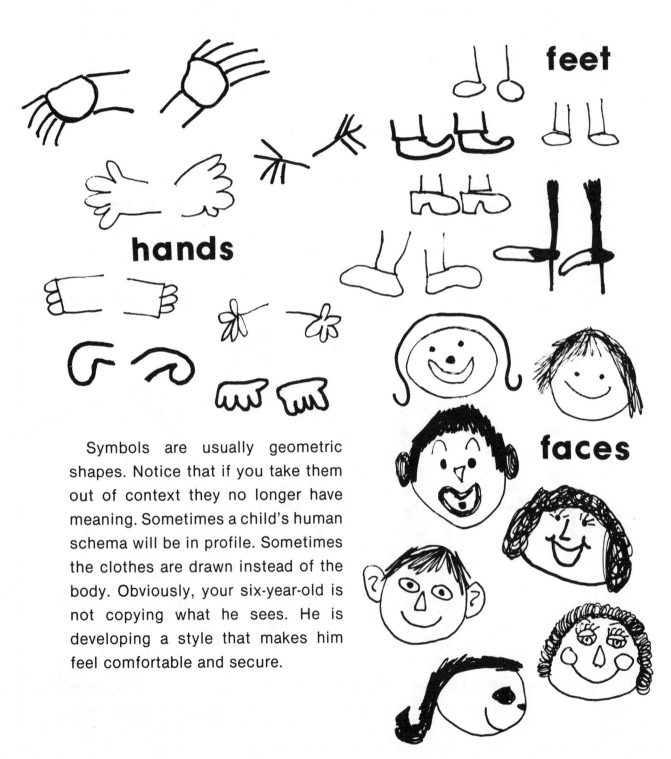

Symbols are usually geometric shapes. Notice that if you take them out of context they no longer have meaning. Sometimes a child's human schema will be in profile. Sometimes the clothes are drawn instead of the body. Obviously, your six-year-old is not copying what he sees. He is developing a style that makes him feel comfortable and secure.

SPACE SCHEMA

Preschool children are egocentric. When they draw, images may float around the paper with no relation to each other. You can tell when a child has crossed over into the schematic stage, because he has discovered—Ta-Dah!—the BASE LINE! Now he is beginning to see relationships. The tree is on the ground, the grass is on the ground, the house is on the ground, and HE is on the ground. Isn't that comforting? The base line phenomenon is universal and timeless. If you have saved any artwork from your childhood, please look at it. Base line? The base line can be grass, street, or floor, but it has to be. Usually the base line has a partner running parallel to it at the top of the paper. You guessed it—the skyline. To a child, all that space in between is "air." The childish perception of the sky being up is no more of an illusion than the adult perception of the sky being all around. Rather than argue with a schematic child about making the sky meet the ground, you might ask him to fill that empty space with a color, just to make his picture more interesting.

BASE LINE VARIATIONS

Children at this level are so tied to the base line that they will do interesting things to preserve it. For instance, if a child draws a hill or a mountain, he realizes that he can't stretch the line straight across the bottom of the paper. Naturally, he bends it. It's still a base line, because everything on the hill is perpendicular to it, not standing straight.

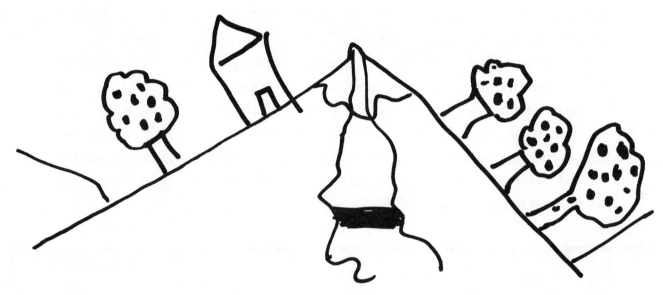

If you could pull on either end of the line, thereby straightening out the mountain, everything would be "correct"—and on a base line. You can see the same thing in drawings of houses. Look at the way chimneys lean over on the roof—bent base line.

Sometimes a child will use more than one base line in an attempt to show depth. After years of doggedly trying to teach first graders that they could show near and far by using several lines at different levels for the ground, I finally gave up. A child convinced me that the concept was beyond first-grade level. She did exactly as I had asked. There were three lines for the ground, one at the bottom of the paper (close-up), one in the middle (middle ground), and one toward the top (background). And over each line was a sky and a sun.

By second and third grade, some children are ready to show depth in their pictures. If you're not sure, explain a little about foreground and background and ask, "Does this make sense to you?" If it doesn't (whatever the concept), put it aside for awhile.

FOLD-OVERS

Drawing both sides of a street or river can present a problem which children may solve by drawing half of the scene upside down. This is called "folding over." If you fold the paper up on either side of the street, for instance, the picture makes sense.

Drawing a table is the same. In this case, if the legs are folded down, it reads correctly. Sometimes the base line is left out altogether, as in a picture of people sitting around a blanket having a picnic or in any depiction of a sporting event. It is not uncommon to see several views in one picture in an attempt by the artist to show everything.

OTHER CHARACTERISTICS OF THE SCHEMATIC STAGE

If a child is inspired to draw about an event, such as "My Vacation" or "Santa Claus Is Coming," he may show several scenes in sequence in the same drawing. Some topics lend themselves to X-ray pictures, which show both the inside and outside of something. "Playing in the Barn" or "Riding Through a Tunnel" might elicit the X-ray response.

At this stage, the use of color has changed from anything goes to a rigid perception of the "correct" color. The sky is blue, the grass is green, the sun is yellow. Color usage may not be the same for every child. Each bases his choice on his most vivid experiences. So if a child remembers an orange sun at twilight, his suns will always be orange. When a child has discovered that he can copy the color of something, he is not anxious to learn about shades and variations.

At this age children are intuitively good designers. Because of the repetition of their schema, their pictures have a natural rhythm. The schematic child also has a sense of composition, positioning the parts of a picture in an interesting way on the paper.

VARIATIONS IN THE SCHEMA

The schema is a comfortable tool, but it shouldn't become a crutch. It is the teacher's job to motivate children to keep their symbols flexible. Through motivation, a child may exaggerate, change, or omit parts of his schema to fit the situation. I like to do a lesson with first graders in which they draw a tree, then look at, feel, and talk about a tree, and draw a tree again. The first drawing is the child's schema for tree; the second, a drawing that shows much more awareness of a tree—its texture, colors, shape.

MOTIVATION AND EVALUATION

Motivation is the key to a successful art experience. Unmotivated children do not get involved and do not care about their work. Highly motivated children are eager to begin, try their hardest, are often still busy when it's time to clean up, and are proud of their finished work. Motivating a class is a little like going on stage. You have to be enthusiastic, sometimes dramatic, sometimes goofy. Children at this age can't just be told. They have to experience. Motivation can take different forms, depending on what you  are trying to teach. Use stories and poems, music, costumes, props, slides or reproductions of famous works of art, or a new medium. All can be motivational. Sometimes a brainstorming session with ideas listed on the board helps get the children revved up. There is a magic moment when it's time to begin working. Too much talk can kill the inspiration.

Children tend to "fiddle" if materials are right there in front of them. Motivation might take place in another part of the room, so that the working area is ready when the children are; or part of the materials can be passed out in advance, reserving only those things that might cause problems.

After the initial motivational period, you need to see each child to further encourage, answer questions, keep on task, and evaluate.

Evaluation needn't be anything spectacular. You might comment on interesting things that are happening on various papers while the class is still working, or children may volunteer to share their work at the end of the period. By third grade you can try a modified critique, in which everybody's picture is stuck on the board and the class discusses them. "Modified" because we don't want heavy criticism—mostly comments on what was done well in each picture, with a few suggestions here and there about how the work could be improved. Children are not fooled by constant praise. It is meaningless if it isn't warranted or sincerely given. Here are some sample comments:

"I like this section, because it is bright and full of action. This corner looks empty. Can you think of something to fill the space?"

"Oh, I thought that was a cat. If it is supposed to be a rabbit you need to make the ears a little longer. Then people will know what animal you intended it to be."

"Your drawing is interesting. You've included a lot of details. But it's so small. Do it again, but make it much bigger this time."

"I know you are getting tired of working on this picture, but hang in there. There are so many good things about it. Don't hurry now and spoil what you've done."

Get the idea? Comments should be specific. Children value your honest opinion. If you give it consistently, your praise is extra special.

A WORD TO PARENTS

The lessons in this book were planned for a classroom situation. There is no reason you can't try them at home with your children, but your approach will need to be different. First, read through all of the activities, so that you'll have several suggestions in mind the next time your kids get the urge to do something creative. Your motivation time should take the form of a discussion about the activity. If your children are anything like mine, they don't think you know nearly as much as a teacher (even if you happen to be a teacher). So rather than going through a long tirade, simply approach each project as a game or problem. You set down the rules, and the children must work within

" WHAT CAN WE DO?"

the boundaries given. Encourage them to keep going and to complete what they begin. Home is much different than school. For some children it provides a better atmosphere for art, because there are fewer distractions. On the other hand, classmates motivate and stimulate each other. At home there aren't as many people to react to and with. At home a child feels more like his own boss. He may not stick to the boundaries of the project. As long as he is involved and creating, don't be too fussy about his bending the rules. Finally, give him your opinion (gently, please) if he asks. Don't try to take over and show him how you would do it. He's a child and you're an adult, two different animals when it comes to picture making.

One last piece of advice. . . establish a cleanup routine or you'll end up doing it yourself. Learning to be responsible for supplies and equipment is as important as doing the art.

HINTS

The following section will give you tips, based on many years of experience, on housekeeping and the technical aspects of teaching art.

GLUING

Glue is messy, especially in the hands of children. Since it is more reliable than paste, just think of it as a necessary evil. Most children can master neat gluing if you consistently remind them how to do it:

1) Touch the tip of the bottle to the paper as you apply the glue.

2) Trace the outline of the shape you are gluing with a thin thread, not a rope of glue.

3) Always (unless told otherwise) put the glue on the piece to be glued down, not on the background paper; or to put it another way, apply glue to the smaller paper.

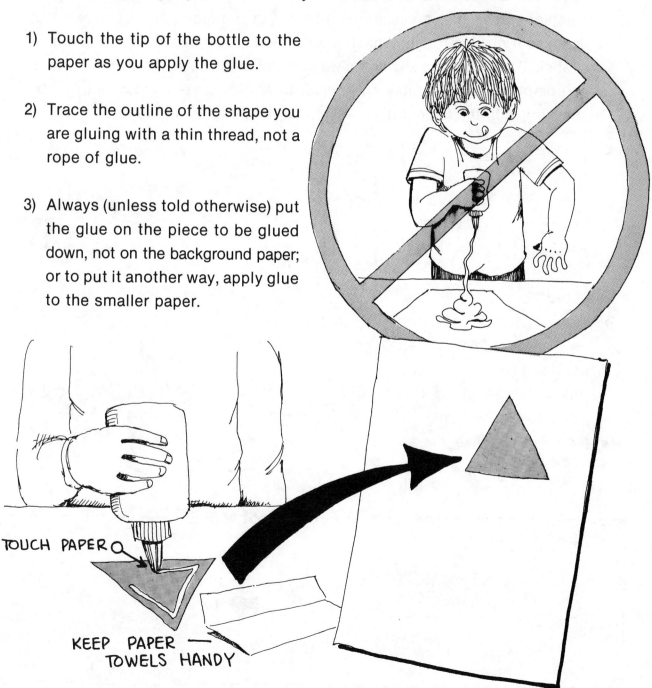

TOUCH PAPER

KEEP PAPER — TOWELS HANDY

CUTTING

Freehand cutting is a good practice. It encourages a playfulness you can't get from drawing. Children have trouble cutting certain shapes. Circles are easier if you start with a square, then cut around the corners. Keep turning the paper as you cut. If a child is particularly vexed over cutting the shape he wants, have him draw it first, then cut. Any time duplicates are needed—four wheels, two eyes, several buttons or polka-dots—teach the children to cut through several layers of paper at once. For instant stripes, hair, grass, tree trunks, fur, or centipede legs, cut a series of slits as if making fringe. Whack across the top end of the slits for a pile of "sticks" to be used in any of the ways mentioned above. If a child is cutting a complicated shape, like an animal, have him break it down into parts, starting with the largest first. Assemble the parts with glue.

PAPER STRIPS

SIMPLIFY ...... ASSEMBLE

BODY

HEAD

TAIL

EAR

TRUNK

LEGS

ELEPHANT !

PAINTING

From first grade on, children should be taught the proper way to care for paints and brushes. The following rules are designed to make painting fun for everybody, especially the teacher.

Dip only the bristles of the brush into the paint. Don't go in up to your elbow! Touch the brush to the inside of the paint container to get rid of the "dribbles."

Rinse the brush well before changing colors. Dip it all the way to the bottom of the water can and jiggle. Avoid stirring the water around and around, because it sloshes out over the edge of the can.

Blot excess water on a paper towel. Never bang the brush on the rim of the water can. Nobody likes paint-water showers.

RINSE

BLOT

DIP into PAINT

Be considerate of the people around you. Refrain from using techniques which are too messy, such as the ever-popular flipping and spattering method of applying color.

15

CLEANUP

A few minutes before cleanup time, begin to notify the class, "Ten more minutes to work . . . five minutes left . . . finish whatever you're doing right now and stop." Assign reliable helpers to collect papers and supplies. Each child is responsible for his own work area. If hand washing is necessary, make sure the other jobs are done first. Cleanup time can drag on and on if you let it. It helps to begin the next activity when most of the class is ready. The stragglers will learn to hurry.

"I APPRECIATE YOUR ENTHUSIASTIC APPROACH TO CLEANING UP, COURTNEY, BUT WE REALLY MUST MOVE ON TO SPELLING YET TODAY."

DEMONSTRATIONS

Sometimes it is necessary to demonstrate the procedures you want the class to follow. To keep children from copying your work, remove it from view after the demonstration. Whenever possible have class members help with the demonstration. Always encourage children to use their own ideas or to use new techniques in their own way.

DRAWING

Most children like to draw and some LOVE to draw. The latter variety go through reams of paper and use up countless markers, pencils, and crayons. As you might expect, those who draw a lot become quite good at it. They fill their pictures with details that others overlook.

All children should be encouraged to draw from memory, from their imagination, and from observation. Drawing helps them become more perceptive, more aware of themselves and their environment. Some children have a natural tendency toward visual expression. For them, drawing is a way of "talking" about things they can't put into words. Of course, before children learn to read and spell, drawing is their **only** means of nonverbal communication. Finally, drawing helps to keep the right brain processes active. Imagination and creative play tend to atrophy during this time when children are learning to read, spell, and figure. Drawing helps keep this from happening.

Between the ages of five and nine, children develop their formulas (schema) for drawing people, animals, houses, trees, cars. If left alone, they will use the schema freely, without much variation. The following drawing activities are designed to help a child go beyond his set symbols, to stretch his imagination and powers of observation. The lessons will also help the teacher (or parent) to motivate and help a student with his drawings.

DRAW A HOUSE

2nd-3rd Grades

pencils, erasers, 12″ x 18″ white drawing paper, drawing boards (workbooks or magazines will do), viewfinders (large index cards with 1½″ x 1″ holes cut in the centers)

Since this activity takes place outside, before you begin tell the children exactly where they are allowed to go to draw. It is much easier to keep track of them if they are contained.

Tell the class that the drawings must come from observation. Making up things is not allowed; however, omissions may be made at the discretion of the artist. Explain that by holding a viewfinder in front of his face, and closing one eye, an artist can focus in on what he wants to draw. Moving the viewfinder closer to the face creates a bigger field of vision; moving it farther away, narrows the view.

The first thing each child should do when he goes outside is to look at several houses through his viewfinder until he finds one he likes. He should think for himself. Drawing takes concentration. Warn children not to sit with people who will bother them by talking too much.

Once the houses are decided on, drawing can begin. Tell the students to start with a door or window, to draw it carefully, including as much detail as possible. Then they should look to the left and right of the starting point, continuing to draw exactly what they see. They should pay careful attention to relationships. How far is the window from the door? Are windows and doors even with each other at the roofline? How tall is the house? Does the roof appear to be at least as tall as the lower half of the house? How much space between the windows and the edges of the house? What is the house made of? Does it look different from the roof material? How can you show this? What is above the house? Next to it? In front of it?

These questions should be pondered before going out, then reiterated, on an individual basis, while work is in progress. Helping your students draw will fine-tune your own perception!

Although some students will rush and others become frustrated, a few will get so involved in their drawings that they will beg to work on them at recess.

When everyone is finished, tape all the drawings on the board. (You needn't be neat about it—just get them up where all can see.) Take a few minutes to talk about why some drawings are especially good and why others are lacking. Stimulation from peers can be a great motivator for the next drawing session.

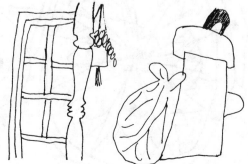

DRAW A BIKE

2nd-3rd Grades

pencils, black fine-point markers, erasers, 12″ x 18″ white drawing paper, two bicycles

Ask two students who ride their bikes to school to wheel them into the classroom. Use two bikes so that the students can get a good view of one or the other, and so they can choose the style they prefer.

Set the bicycles up on a table or counter where they can be seen. Place them so that the sprocket side of the bike is facing the students. Prop the front wheel of each bike to keep it from turning. The students need a straight side view.

Now pose the following questions for discussion:

Is the space between the wheels as big as the diameter of a wheel?

Where is the seat? How high is it in relation to the wheels and to the handlebars?

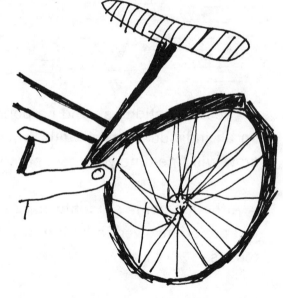

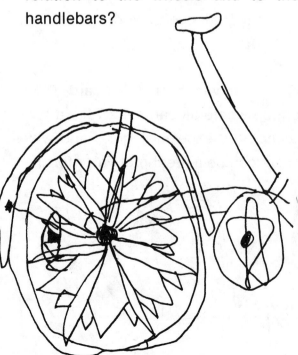

Where is the sprocket in relation to the wheels? How big is it? Do the centers of the front and back wheels and the center of the sprocket all line up?

From your vantage point, does one end of the handlebar look higher than the other? How is the handlebar attached to the bike?

Look at the frame. How are the wheels, seat, and the sprocket attached?

Tell the students to draw one of the bicycles exactly the way they see it. If anyone asks to draw another bike from memory, tell him no. Today the learning comes from careful observation.

Students should draw with pencil. If a sharper, more contrasting drawing is desired, pencil lines can be traced over with a fine-point black marker. Scenery may be added to complete the picture, but no color. This time interest has to come from good drawing.

Hang up the finished drawings after trimming off excess paper. Trimming helps to accentuate the positive and often helps the overall design of the page. Most artists "crop" from time to time. If a student asks why part of his picture is missing, take the opportunity to explain about editing. It's not unlike editing writing. Cropping gets rid of the chaff.

TRAINS

1st-2nd Grades

6″ x 18″ or 6″ x 24 ″ white drawing paper, black fine-point markers, crayons, opaque projector, pictures of engines and individual train cars. A good resource is *The Big Book of Real Trains* by George J. Zaffo (text by Elizabeth Cameron).

Since it is impossible for most classes to view and draw a train on the spot, this approach will suffice. Tell the children that while sometimes it is okay to draw from the imagination, today it is not. They will be looking at a train, one car at a time. They are to draw what they see, including as much detail as they can. They will begin with the most complex part, the engine. Project two or three pictures of steam engines on the wall, using the opaque projector. You should be able to find examples in the encyclopedia. Point out the simple shapes and have the children name them: boiler, rectangle; smokestack, rectangle; cowcatcher, triangle; wheels, circles; cab, square; window, square. Finding familiar shapes to begin with makes the engine less formidable. Tell everyone to decide which way his train will be traveling; then draw the

BEGIN WITH SIMPLE SHAPES

engine at the very beginning of the paper. The paper is so long, some of it will always be trailing off one side of the desk or the other. Since this is a lesson in observation, caution the students not to draw ahead. If anyone finishes a car with time to spare, he must wait until the next car is projected before drawing some more. As each car is shown, call attention to its unique features. For instance, the cattle car has open places between the boards so that the animals can breathe, but the refrigerator car is tight and has heavy hinges and bolts on the door to keep the produce inside cold. Drawing curved instead of straight lines at the ends of the tank car will help make it look like a cylinder. Do the children notice that the cars have two sets of front and back wheels?

Show four or five cars, then the caboose. If some children are running out of room, they may want to omit a car and save room for the caboose. Allow several minutes for each car (3-5), gauging the time by the amount of detail on a car. Move to the next one when most children are ready.

After you have shown all the cars, allow time for the kids to go back and finish details they may not have had time for earlier. They should also draw tracks, smoke, ground, sky, trees, crossing gates. Finally, they should color the trains. If time is short, store the drawings on an accessible table or shelf, and tell the students to work on them in their spare time.

TOOT! TOOT! All aboard the train bound for better observation skills through drawing!

TREE HOUSE

3rd Grade

9″ x 12″ white drawing paper, 12″ x 18″ white drawing paper, viewfinder (see Draw a House, page 18), pencil, fine-point permanent black markers, watercolors, water, paper towels

Plan to spend two or three class periods on this activity. To begin, the students will go outside to draw a tree. They should work in pencil on the 9″ x 12″ paper. Take along workbooks to use for drawing boards. Tell them they must each choose a particular tree to look at and try to draw it realistically. Viewfinders will help students focus on a tree while masking out distractions. Discuss briefly the way a tree grows—from a large base to smaller and smaller divisions as the branches split off from the trunk. Leaves are not important at this point in the drawing.

After 15-20 minutes, call everyone into the school building. If possible, read the class the poem "Tree House" from Shel Silverstein's *Where the Sidewalk Ends.* Ask the kids to tell you what the perfect tree house would be like. Write their ideas on the board. If the discussion bogs down, a few questions will get it going again. How would you get into the tree house? Would there be any kind of communications system? What would you do in a tree house? Who would be allowed in? Would you have any furniture? Let imaginations have free reign. When the chalkboard is full of ideas, hand out the 12″ x 18″ drawing paper. The students are now to enlarge the drawings of the trees. They should make whatever alterations necessary, so that the enlarged tree can accommodate the tree house of their dreams. If a student is having trouble, help him find in his original sketch a possible tree house

site. Most students will take off with no problems. Some may come up with multi or split-level designs. As they are working, remind them to show how entrance is gained. Encourage them to draw the building materials in detail—boards, nails, pulleys, ladders, ropes. They may now draw leaves, designing them to add to the coziness of the tree house. As artists have done throughout history, each student will have to invent his own way of drawing foliage. One child may indicate individual leaves, while another may draw the shape of the bunch. Scribbling should be avoided—it is thoughtless.

At the next session, allow time for everyone to complete the pencil drawing. It should then be retraced with fine-point marker. (Make sure the marker is permanent or the ink will run when water colors are added.) Before painting begins, talk with the kids about the feeling they get when they're up in a tree. How does the sun look when it filters through the leaves? Do they want the picture to have a sunny day look or a gray, drizzly atmosphere? To achieve an airy sky, wet the paper before painting. Use blue and yellow, as well as green, to show shadows and light on the leaves.

Perhaps each child could write an original poem or composition to display with his tree house painting.

"A tree house,
 a free house,
A secret you-and-
 me house. . . ."

CASTLES

3rd Grade

12″ x 18″ white drawing paper; 12″ x 18″ newsprint; pencil; pictures of castles (slides or photographs in books), *Cathedral* and *Castle* by David Macaulay; black, felt-tipped markers in fine and extra fine points; scratch paper

Drawing teaches. Through drawing, children can experience other times and places. They can explore and wonder and dream in their drawings. This project is designed for that purpose. As a bonus, your students will learn pena and ink techniques as well.

Begin by looking at lots of pictures of castles and parts of castles. Discuss the unusual features you notice—towers, arrow loops, portcullis. How? What? Why? Why were the castle walls built thicker at the bottom? How did an arrow loop work? What did the portcullis do? What would it have been like to live in a castle? Why were battlements needed? To help the students understand what medieval life was like, read to them from David Macaulay's *Castle.* (The March 1983, issue of *Cricket Magazine* has several articles about castle life that the children would find interesting.) You must capture them totally.

Before beginning a final drawing, allow the kids time to make a collection of sketches of details from various castles you've shown them. Tell them they are to use the sketches to design castles. Each might pretend that he is royalty and must decide on a location and a plan for his own castle. He should think about the site so that it can be indicated in the background. From a design standpoint, it is best not to place the castle at the very bottom of the paper. Allow the viewer a little space.

Technical problems will arise. A few children will not know where to begin. The best place is the front door. Draw a rectangle. Draw a battlement on it. Add a tower on the left and a colonnade on the right. Put in windows and arrow loops. What about the door? Would it look like your own front door? How would it be different? Is your castle on a hill? Near the water? Have these slow starters scratch around on their sketch papers, trying different combinations of towers and rectangles until they feel confident enough to start on the final drawing. Some students will want to show a drawbridge over a moat. Give them a short lesson in perspective and demonstrate on a scrap of paper. (See illustrations.) Encourage everyone to use overlap in placing towers.

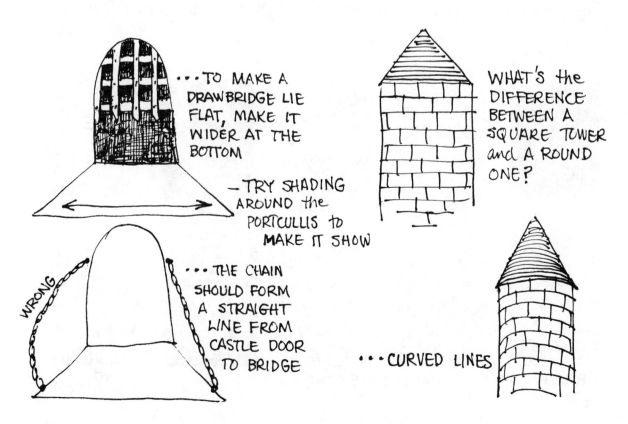

... TO MAKE A DRAWBRIDGE LIE FLAT, MAKE IT WIDER AT THE BOTTOM

— TRY SHADING AROUND the PORTCULLIS to MAKE IT SHOW

WRONG

... THE CHAIN SHOULD FORM A STRAIGHT LINE FROM CASTLE DOOR TO BRIDGE

WHAT'S the DIFFERENCE BETWEEN A SQUARE TOWER and A ROUND ONE?

... CURVED LINES

When the pencil drawings have been finished, launch into the second part of the project, using markers for texture and shading. Compare the drawings to cake. As they are, they are like cake without frosting. The addition of marker will make them "richer." Prepare several small sheets of paper showing various ways to shade. (See examples.) Tell the students that scribbling will not be tolerated. Look at the illustrations in Macaulay's books. Notice how he draws stone, brick, clouds, water, wood. Learn from him. Give everyone a piece of scratch paper to experiment on. After they have tried several ways of shading and practiced drawing the textures they want to use, they should return to the castle drawings. First, retrace all of the pencil lines with marker; then proceed to shading and drawing textures.

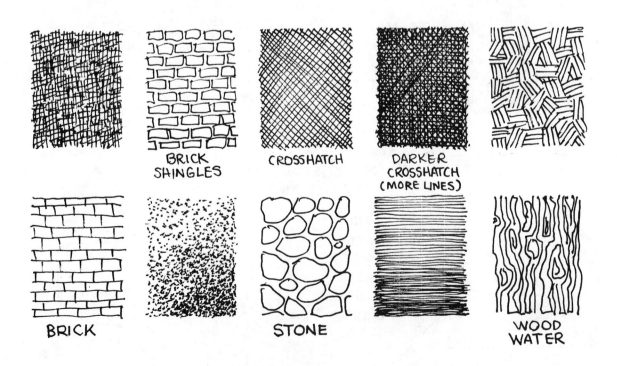

BRICK SHINGLES   CROSSHATCH   DARKER CROSSHATCH (MORE LINES)

BRICK   STONE   WOOD WATER

Experiment with different point sizes. Variety in the size of the lines makes a drawing interesting. This is tedious work, but the results are stunning. If possible, let the students work on their drawings for short periods of time over several days.

With castle drawings all around, now would be a good time to read about Robin Hood or King Arthur and the Knights of the Round Table. Won't the kids be surprised to find out that there were others before He-Man and the Castle Greyskull?

LANDSCAPE DRAWING

2nd-3rd Grades

12″ x 18″ white drawing paper, crayons, reproductions of landscapes by Grandma Moses (can be found in books of her works)

Grandma Moses' story is an interesting one. Here is a brief background to share with your class before looking at her pictures.

Grandma Moses was born shortly before Lincoln became President. She grew up on a farm. Her maiden name was Robertson—Anna Mary Robertson. When she was twenty-one she marrried Robert Moses. They had ten children, five of whom lived to adulthood. Anna had always liked to draw. When she was little, she and her brothers painted with berry juice! She didn't have much time for art after she had a family, but after her children grew up and her husband died, she found herself with nothing to do. She began to paint scenes that she remembered from her childhood. A gallery dealer saw her paintings and organized a show. Before long she was well-known as Grandma Moses, primitive painter. (A "primitive" is an artist who never had any formal training.) She lived to be 101 years old.

Show the class several of Moses' landscapes. Ask the children to name what they see. Write the word *landscape* on the board. How can you tell that Grandma Moses' landscapes are based on her memories of the past? Are the pictures interesting? Why? One reason she was able to paint so much in one painting was that she made the ground go almost to the top of the picture. Have a student point to something that appears to be very far away. Have someone else point to something close up. What did Grandma Moses

do to create the illusion of close up and far away? There are two things to remember: size and position. Something close up must be larger and lower

BOTH SIZE _and_ POSITION ARE IMPORTANT. THE SMALLER HOUSE DOES NOT LOOK FARAWAY. IT JUST LOOKS LIKE A SMALLER HOUSE!

OOPS! FLYING HOUSE! ANOTHER GROUND LINE IS NEEDED TO INDICATE FARAWAY.

on the paper. Something faraway must be smaller and higher up. That's why Grandma Moses always made the ground up so high—something has to hold up those faraway trees and houses!

Ask each student to draw a landscape from memory or imagination. Review things that can go into a landscape: ground, sky, roads, fences, buildings, trees, ponds or rivers, fields, animals, people, traffic. Tell them to try an experiment. Instead of drawing the ground at the bottom of the paper, put it up high like Grandma Moses did. Try to show something close up and something faraway. Remember, all the space in between is ground. Fill it with lots of interesting details.

As the children are working, help individuals who are having trouble. Ask the whole class to think about the time of year, the time of day, and the weather they want to show in their landscapes.

Don't be surprised to find some children still tied to the base line concept. This lesson is an attempt to push them a step beyond, and many are ready. The drawings will be far from "correct," but no matter. You have made the kids think. What they lack in accuracy, they make up for in inventiveness.

DRAWING, ROUAULT STYLE

2nd-3rd Grades

12″ x 18″ manilla drawing paper (use old paper if you have it, because there will be some waste), black crayon, watercolors, water, paper towels, table covers, reproduction of *The Old King* by Georges Rouault (this should be in any comprehensive book on Rouault's work)

Pass out paper, and have students take out a black crayon. Look at Rouault's king. Does it look like a photograph? Why not? How is Rouault's style different from other artists? Try to get the kids to see that Rouault used mainly primary colors and heavy black outlines. He was not interested in being a camera. He wanted to express himself in his own way. Rouault worked for a time in a stained glass factory. Perhaps his style has something to do with that experience.

Tell the children that they will see what it is like to draw boldly with black crayon, taking both style and subject matter from Rouault. Have them begin with a large oval on the lengthwise paper. Press hard and make strong, dark marks. Before drawing the features, have everyone do research on his own face. Place the thumb next to the eye and the middle finger on top of the head. Holding that measurement, place the middle finger next to the eye. The thumb should rest on the chin, proving that eyes are in the middle of the head. Nose and mouth are then spaced between eyes and chin. Ears are about even with eyes at the top and nose at the bottom. The neck joins onto the head behind the ears. It is not as wide as the head, but it is not terribly skinny, either.

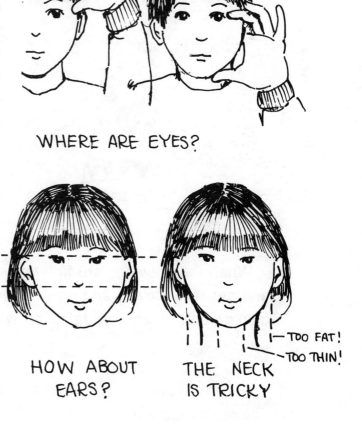

WHERE ARE EYES?

HOW ABOUT EARS?

THE NECK IS TRICKY

←TOO FAT!
←TOO THIN!

Have the children continue to draw, adding eyes, nose, mouth, eyebrows, hair, crown, beard, neck, shoulders, jewels, whatever they choose to make the king their own. The only thing they **MUST** do is draw firmly with the black crayon. Hair may be colored in solidly. Ask the artists to think about the expression a king would have on his face. A silly grin? Hardly. If a child makes an irreversible mistake and has used both sides of the paper, give him a new piece. Have him keep the old one to experiment on.

by Phillip

by Jill

by Sharon

by Georges

When the drawings are finished, students should take out watercolors and get table covers and cans of water. They should paint both king and background. If an area is to be white, it should be colored with white crayon.

For a finishing touch, crop the royal portraits slightly, and mount them on colored construction paper.

MACHINES

1st Grade

12″ x 18″ white drawing paper, fine-point black markers, "machine parts" (see NOTE), crayons, *The Sleep Book* or *The Sneetches* by Dr. Seuss or "The Homework Machine" found in Shel Silverstein's *A Light in the Attic*

NOTE: Before presenting this lesson, assemble several "Machine-making Kits" (one for every four or five children). Make cardboard templates of cogs, wheels, flags, plumbing pipes—see illustrations for ideas. Put these into envelopes to be handed out when the children are ready to begin drawing. If you want more permanent templates, cut them out of plastic lids.

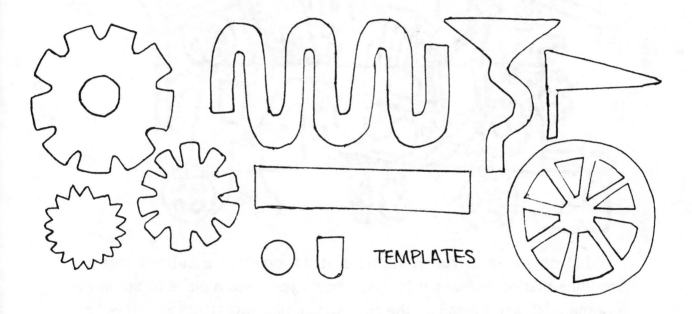

TEMPLATES

Machines are so common in our society that children are hardly impressed or intimidated by them. To jog their imaginations, read pertinent parts from one or two of the stories suggested. Show the illustrations of the imaginary machines and discuss the unusual parts—chutes, steam pipes, lights, conveyor belts, tubes, wires. If you have any pictures of real machines, show them, too.

By now the kids will be anticipating your question: What kind of machine would you invent if you could make one to do a-a-a-anything you wanted? If the responses are fairly ordinary at first, encourage them to use their imaginations. They might think of machines which could do some kind of work or machines which make something. The machine's purpose would affect its design. Steer away from the robot, a fairly stereotypic image. The following comments from you will help get the discussion going along the desired lines.

What jobs do you hate doing that a machine could help you with? What kinds of parts would it need to do the jobs?

What do you wish you could have at the press of a button? Invent a machine that could make it for you. Would you need a place to put in the raw materials and a place for the product to come out? Could you show how the machine does its work?

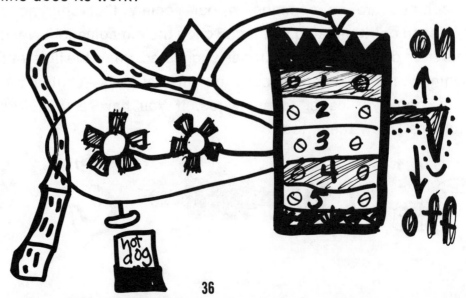

36

What if you wanted to shrink or enlarge something? What would it be? (Somebody will say he wants to shrink his big sister. Don't let the discussion get morbid.)

After explaining the kits and showing the children the parts, pass them out. They can use whatever parts they choose to help them get started. They should draw with the markers. When their ideas begin to take shape, they should feel free to add parts of their own design. Many children begin with nothing in particular in mind, and some may change their minds several times about their machine's function. No matter, they are inventing! You are bound to have one or two slow starters. Sadly, even in first grade some children are too literal to know how to be outlandish. Try to get these individuals to decide on either a making or doing machine; then help them figure out what parts would be needed. If nothing else, begin with a switch to turn the machine on. Each child should decide if he wants to color his machine. Some may want to color only certain parts.

As the drawings progress, the children will become more and more verbal. The machines are a natural for a creative writing project. Display the drawings and writing together.

THE FIGURE

Knowledge of the human figure and skill in its portrayal are basic to art at any level. During the primary years, we are not looking for perfect proportion or realism. This is the age of the schema, remember. The main concern should be detail. How much is a student aware of, and how well is he able to depict what he sees and knows? We want to influence the schema and keep it flexible through a variety of approaches to the figure. The next pages give you several figure-study activities.

THAT'S ME!

1st-2nd Grades

12″ x 18″ drawing paper, crayons

This figure-drawing lesson is a good one to use at the beginning of the school year. It reveals the levels of maturity (and immaturity) in the class, puts the children at ease and helps you learn a bit about them, and sets the stage for future art projects.

After telling the class that they are going to think about how people look, how they are alike and how they are different, have everyone stand. Ask them to name with you the parts of the body as you point them out. Start with the head.

To emphasize the importance of necks, have the children hunch their shoulders up around their ears. Everybody count to ten together and listen to the way they sound.

After naming shoulders, arms, and fingers, ask if anyone knows what the part between the shoulders and hips is called. Somebody will say "body." Tell the class that artists call this part the "torso." Ask what shape a torso is. Kind of a rectangle, isn't it? What holds the torso up? Legs. Then come feet, and that's how people look the same.

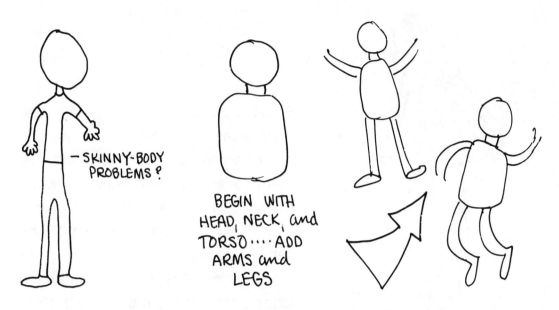

-SKINNY-BODY PROBLEMS?

BEGIN WITH HEAD, NECK, and TORSO·····ADD ARMS and LEGS

How do they look different? Why don't you look just like the person next to you? After all, you have the same parts.

Keep the discussion going until the children have mentioned these differences: hair color, hair style (straight, curly, long, short, part, bangs, ponytails, barrettes), eye color, skin color, clothing, freckles, teeth missing, glasses. Ask them who has new shoes, who is wearing stripes, who has a belt on, whose jeans have a patch. . . .

Pass out the drawing paper. It must be placed lengthwise. Tell the children they are to draw a picture of themselves. They should begin with a head no smaller than an orange (indicate by framing the size with your fingers) and try to make the person as tall as the paper. Remember to include all the parts—that show when we are dressed. If you don't put that last phrase in, you may have an embarrassing situation. Thinking about how everybody looks different, make the person look like you.

Not all children will draw the clothes they are wearing but encourage them to try. As they are working, remind them further by saying things like, "Oh, good! I see Jane remembered to draw her fingers." Have them become more aware of the color of skin by placing their hands next to the paper. People aren't black or white, but shades. Urge them to color their skin.

Some kids will color everything but their faces, for some reason. As you see children beginning to finish, tell them to add scenery—sky, flowers, trees, perhaps a pet. Those who didn't make it to the bottom of the paper might think of something for the person to stand on—a hill, rock, ladder. When it is almost time to stop, review the body parts one more time.

A wide range of ability in drawing and perception will be evident as you evaluate these drawings. The results will help you determine who needs help. You may want to put the pictures away until the end of the school year, then repeat the lesson. It's fun for the children to see if they have changed their way of drawing, and you can check for progress in the use of schema.

SKELETONS

1st-2nd Grades

construction paper: 12″ x 18″ black, 6″ x 9″ white, and 4½″ x 6″ orange; glue; scissors; black crayon

Ask the children if any of them have discovered that certain bones are so close to the skin that they can easily be felt. Have them take turns telling where these bones are, and have everybody find them on themselves. Some that will be mentioned: wrist, fingers, knees, elbows, head (yes, we are all boneheads!), shins, back, and ribs. Take a minute to talk about the cage inside everybody and why it has to be there. Make sure that everybody agrees that we need bones for support and that bones are rigid; then ask, "How many bones do you think there are between the shoulder and the hand, one long one or more than one?"

"Let's suppose there is just one long bone. Everybody make a stiff arm. Now try to eat a bowl of cereal. What? You can't get the spoon to your mouth?"

This demonstration is funny, and it proves that arms have more than one bone. Ask the children to point to the place where the bones meet. As they are showing you their elbows, tell them that the place where two bones meet is called a "joint." Go through the same kind of routine with the legs. Have the kids stand and try to sit without bending their knees. Finally, ask if anyone knows what all the bones together are called. A skeleton, of course.

Tape a piece of black paper on the board. Tell the class you are cutting a shape to represent the head bone or skull. Glue it to the black. Show the children how they can cut long strips of white to use for bones. The strips can then be cut any length. Glue a strip under the skull to represent the backbone. Stick three or four short strips across the backbone for ribs.

(Note: This is one time when it's easier to put the glue on the background paper rather than the pieces being glued. Stress "thin threads of glue.")

Now ask for a volunteer to take **two** strips of paper and make **one** arm. It should look like it is bending. With your own arms, demonstrate several different ways arms can bend. Let a student glue the arm in place. Have the whole class put their arms in the position illustrated. Do the same thing with one leg. Before the children begin to work, tell them that each arm and leg must have two bones and must show movement. They should begin with skull, backbone, and ribs. Remove your sample from the board. As an afterthought, ask them what they could do with the orange paper. Make pumpkins or jack-o'-lanterns! This adds another dimension. The skeleton could be running through a pumpkin patch, juggling jack-o'-lanterns, sitting on a pumpkin, carrying one on his head. . . the children will think of other possibilities.

As the period progresses, keep restating the rule: two bones for each arm and two for each leg. If a child wants to make more than one skeleton, that's fine. Some may have time to add finger and toe bones. The black crayon can be used to draw faces on skeletons and jack-o'-lanterns.

— SEE IF KIDS CAN IMITATE THEIR SKELETON CREATIONS —

These papers make an eye-catching Halloween bulletin board when overlapped so that there are no gaps in the black. Although this activity falls into the category of holiday art, it is not trite, and it does teach a valid lesson in movement of the human figure. In later figure-drawing projects, when you want to encourage action, you can refer to the dancing skeletons.

THE FIGURE IN MOTION: TWO APPROACHES

3rd Grade

Knowing how to draw a person is one thing; making it live and move is another. Many times people pictures look stiff, and they will remain so, unless you make the children think about the way people move their arms, legs, and bodies. Two ways you might go about it are described here.

GESTURE (SCRIBBLE) DRAWING

12″ x 18″ newsprint, black crayon

You will need to try this yourself a few times, so you can demonstrate it for your class. The idea is to capture the movement or gesture of your model. Keep the crayon in continuous motion and work quickly. You should be able to complete a drawing in thirty seconds. Have a student pose for you, and show the class how it is done. Stress that the movement is important, not the face, not the clothes. Let children take turns posing for each other. Have the model go through a complete action, such as shooting a basket; then do it again, freezing when the pose looks interesting. As they are drawing, encourage the children to notice how the arms and legs are bent, whether the back is straight or leaning. Time the poses, beginning with 45-second ones and working down to 20 or 30 seconds. Any kind of sport, including dance and gymnastics, affords a variety of poses. Students should use both sides of their papers and draw rather small. Have more paper available for people who run out of room.

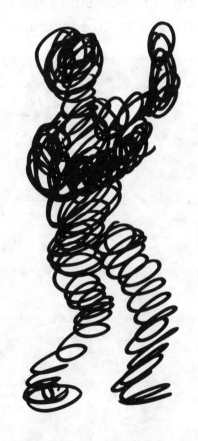

SHADOW PEOPLE

1st-2nd-3rd Grades

12″ x 18″ manilla or newsprint, brushes, paint in a dark color, filmstrip projector, old bed sheet suspended in the middle of the room. It can be draped over a wire or long broom handle. It must touch the floor and be higher than your students' heads.

IF POSSIBLE, GO TO THE MULTI-PURPOSE ROOM···FOLDED LUNCH TABLES WORK WELL to SUSPEND SHEET FROM.

This method makes seeing movement easy, because there is nothing else to distract. The model stands behind the "screen" with the light from the projector shining on his back. Experiment to see how far away the projector needs to be from the model. The model should stand quite close to the screen. The children should work quickly, drawing with their brushes the image of the shadow before them. They should work fairly small, fitting several poses on one page. In order for everyone to see, it would be a good idea to have the class sit in a large semicircle on the floor around the screen. Let every two children share a small container of thick paint. When it is time to stop, have them put their brushes in a can of water and pick up the paint containers. Have damp towels handy for wiping up drips.

FOLLOW-UP

12″ x 18″ white drawing paper; chalkboard chalk; oil crayons; reproductions or pictures in books of paintings by Leroy Nieman, George Bellows (boxers), and Edgar Degas (ballerinas)

If you want the children to do a finished picture, show them examples of the work of the artists named above. The figure in motion does have a history! Draw attention to the different style of each artist. Ask the kids to think about the people who draw their favorite super heroes. These artists

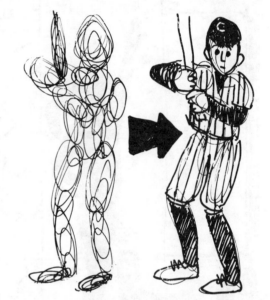

must know how to make their characters move. Hand out the figure studies, and ask everyone to pick out two or three poses they like. On a clean sheet of paper they should enlarge the chosen figures with chalk. They should work lightly and avoid building up too much chalk dust on the paper. When the gestures of the figures have been established, they can be colored with oil crayon. Now the artists need to slow down and even do a little research, if necessary, into team colors and uniforms. The scribbled or shadow people should begin to look "real." Some students may choose to keep their figures small and draw an entire team. Others will prefer to draw one large person. When the figures are colored, some kind of background will complete the picture. There is room for variety here, too. Of course, the first thing that comes to mind is a

playing field. Other possibilities: bright colors, radiating out from the figure, a poster look with the team's name worked into the design, the use of line and color to accentuate the movement of the figure(s).

PAPER PEOPLE

1st-2nd-3rd Grades

6″ x 9″ or 9″ x 12″ (for large figures) construction paper in a variety of colors, glue, scissors, crayons or markers

Let the students select three pieces of paper, one for a shirt, one for pants or skirt, and one for the head and hands. They will put together a person by starting with the clothes. Direct the entire class in cutting shirts and pants on the fold, according to the diagrams. Show how to cut dresses and skirts for those who want to begin that way.

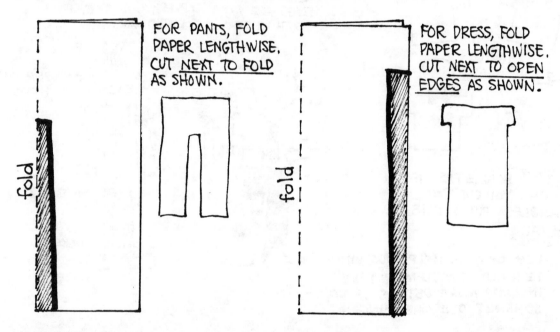

FOR PANTS, FOLD PAPER LENGTHWISE. CUT <u>NEXT TO FOLD</u> AS SHOWN.

FOR DRESS, FOLD PAPER LENGTHWISE. CUT <u>NEXT TO OPEN EDGES</u> AS SHOWN.

FOR SHORT and LONG-SLEEVED SHIRTS and SKIRTS, FOLD PAPER SHORTWISE. CUT AS SHOWN.

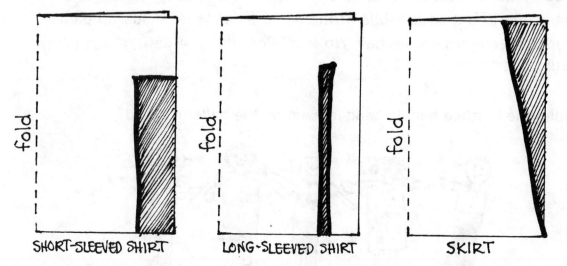

SHORT-SLEEVED SHIRT   LONG-SLEEVED SHIRT   SKIRT

At this point work should cease for a discussion period. How will these clothes become people? What is missing? As children offer suggestions, make a list on the board. To demonstrate the importance of a big-enough head, cut out one that is way too small and hold it up to one of the kid's shirt and pants. At the same time remind them to add a neck. It can be cut all in one piece with the head or attached with glue. Encourage the children to observe their own and their classmates' clothing. They should add as many details as possible to make the paper person interesting. Use paper scraps, crayon, or marker for details.

—TOO SMALL!   —NO NECK

TURTLE HEAD   —GOOD!

EYES ARE MORE EXPRESSIVE IF THEY HAVE BOTH WHITE and COLORED PARTS

—HAT
—COLLAR CUT
—TIE
BELT—

—BOW
—PAPER STRIP HAIR
—ROUNDED SLEEVES
—BUTTONS
SOCKS!

BOW IS EASY IF YOU CUT TWO TRIANGLES, PUT POINTS TOGETHER

IT'S OKAY TO HELP KIDS WITH TECHNICAL PROBLEMS··· THEY'LL INCLUDE MORE DETAILS IF DOING SO IS NOT OVERWHELMING.

Now, back to work! Circulate, offering suggestions and help when needed. Continue to mention ideas to the whole class to keep them thinking: "Remember to cut both hands at the same time! What holds up pants? Paper strips might work for hair. No feet? Poor thing. A hat! What a good idea!"

Hang the finished people hand-in-hand on the bulletin board.

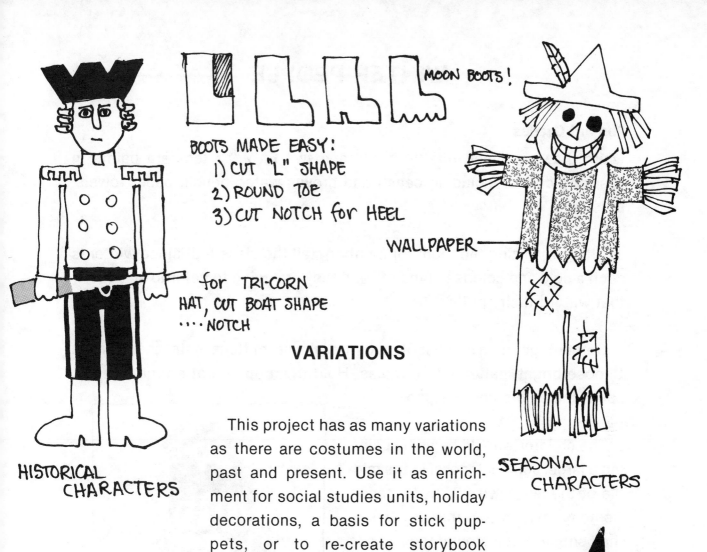

MOON BOOTS!

BOOTS MADE EASY:
1) CUT "L" SHAPE
2) ROUND TOE
3) CUT NOTCH for HEEL

for TRI-CORN
HAT, CUT BOAT SHAPE
····NOTCH

WALLPAPER

VARIATIONS

This project has as many variations as there are costumes in the world, past and present. Use it as enrichment for social studies units, holiday decorations, a basis for stick puppets, or to re-create storybook characters. See the illustrations for ideas.

HISTORICAL CHARACTERS

SEASONAL CHARACTERS

YARN HAIR

UNIFORMS of DIFFERENT PROFESSIONS

STORYBOOK CHARACTERS

HOLIDAY CHARACTERS

WINTER PEOPLE

2nd-3rd Grades

white drawing paper, one 9″ x 12″ and two 6″ x 9″; tempera paints in assorted colors, including peach and brown; water; pencil; paper towels; brushes

After organizing the room for painting, tell the class that since winter is such a cold and colorless time of year, they are going to get into an activity that will lift their spirits.

Gather together a number of students' gloves, mittens, hats, and scarves. Choose bright, patterned examples. Hold them up one at a time and talk about the colors and designs.

The children should begin by painting a large, solid-color oval in the middle of the lengthwise 9″ x 12″ paper. Demonstrate. While this is drying, they should trace around their hands on the two smaller sheets of paper. They may draw around the fingers to make gloves, or bunch them together to make mittens. The kids can help each other draw around their writing hands. As they begin to paint the gloves and mittens, remind them to use designs and patterns.

They need not be too careful about staying in the lines, because everything will be cut out later.

When the faces are dry, features, hair, hats, and scarves can be added. Again, go for pizzazz—zigzags, stripes, checks, polka-dots! Warn the painters to use small, fairly dry brushes when painting facial features. Too much water now can spell disaster.

SESSION TWO

Wear a ski sweater today or bring along a couple of winter apparel catalogues. Taking the chance that one of your students will be wearing a ski sweater is a little risky. Set up for painting. Give everybody a sheet of white drawing paper 12″ square.

Have the class look at the designs in a ski sweater. Point out the simple shapes which are repeated to create a complex pattern. Note that the design covers certain areas of the sweater while the rest is a solid color. Demonstrate the technique of making a stripe of a solid color, letting it dry, then putting a pattern on top. (Children seem naturally inclined to paint a million polka-dots, then try to fill in a background around them!) Tell the students that they are to fill the paper with ski sweater designs as if they were designing a piece of cloth. Don't worry about the shape of the sweater today. That part will come later. When the paintings are dry, store them with the heads and mittens from the last session.

SESSION THREE

Hand out the papers from the two preceding sessions. Have one painting center set up for those who need to finish. They should do this first, so the paint will be dry by the time they are ready to cut out the pieces. Put out 9″ x 12″ paper in assorted colors to be used for pants and 6″ x 9″ white, red, and black "boot paper." Let the children choose one of the larger size and two of the smaller. Before they begin cutting and assembling the parts, have them all draw the outline of the sweater on the back side of the paper they designed last session. Demonstrate this, and have the kids follow along with you. This may seem a bit dictatorial, but it will save the ruination of many ski sweater designs. It's a technical problem and will not interfere with individual expression. Follow the diagrams.

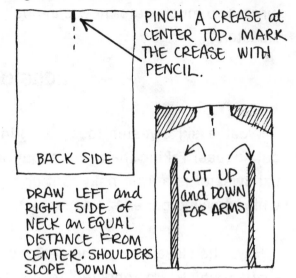

PINCH A CREASE at CENTER TOP. MARK THE CREASE WITH PENCIL.

BACK SIDE

DRAW LEFT and RIGHT SIDE of NECK an EQUAL DISTANCE FROM CENTER. SHOULDERS SLOPE DOWN

CUT UP and DOWN FOR ARMS

Boots can be a problem, too. Both should be cut at the same time. Tell the students to visualize a capital letter *L* hidden in the rectangular paper. Cut away the top corner, leaving the *L*. Now it is a simple matter to round the toe and cut a notch to indicate a heel.

When all the parts have been cut out, they should be assembled with glue. The children will need to get down on the floor to finish these large figures. As each child gets done, staple his paper pal to a bulletin board to get it out of the way. Those who finish first are in charge of cleanup. They can help pick up scraps, empty water, and put away supplies.

These pretty people are too colorful to keep all to yourselves in your room. Hang them in the hall and brighten everybody's day!

CLOWNS

2nd-3rd Grades

white drawing paper (I like to go big on this one) 13" x 24", pencil, black crayon, watercolors, water, paper towels

This lesson takes awhile. Plan to spread it out over two or three sessions. Everybody has seen a clown, whether in person or in a book or on TV. Begin with a brainstorming session. Put three headings on the board: CLOWN FACE, CLOWN SUIT, and CLOWNS HOLD.* Ask the class what makes clowns look different from ordinary people and list ideas under the appropriate headings. Discuss different types of clowns. Some are round and bright, with ruffles and pointed hats. Others are sad. They might wear baggy pants, patches, a squashed hat, and a lo-o-o-ong necktie.

Have the children draw clowns with pencil. Tell them to work big and try to fill the paper. They must use the paper vertically. The clown is the main thing. They should avoid filling in or scribbling areas with the pencil. Show how to outline hair without coloring it. Encourage originality. As they are drawing remind them to think about the types of patterns they might use in the clown's costume—large polka-dots, stripes, checks. Finally, restate some of the ideas on the board.

When a child is satisfied with his pencil drawing, he should trace over all the lines with a black crayon. The crayon has two functions: one, it makes the drawing show up better, and two, it builds a wax "wall" around all the spaces. The crayon needs to be applied heavily. Liken it to mashed potatoes and gravy. If you get a hole in your mashed potatoes, the gravy leaks out. If you don't have a strong wax wall, your watercolors will run into each other!

*List things a clown might carry or hold in his hands.

53

The last step is to paint the clown. When several children are ready, do a demonstration for the whole class. Show them how to get strong color and pale color, how to blot, and how to clean a paint pan that gets dirty. (See Watercolor, page 55). Later, when they begin to work on the background, show them the wet-on-wet technique for getting soft, flowing color. Insist that the background cannot be left white. Ask students to think about the mood they want their paintings to express; then do something to the background that will emphasize that mood.

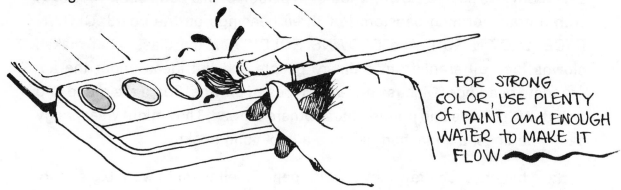

— FOR STRONG COLOR, USE PLENTY OF PAINT and ENOUGH WATER to MAKE IT FLOW

After the paintings have been hung, take a few minutes to discuss them. What have the children done well? Do the colors they chose help to create a sad or happy mood? Have they tried different techniques with their watercolors? If you want to take it one step further, have the kids write about their clowns. Hang the stories or poems under the paintings.

WATERCOLOR TECHNIQUES

Watercolors are versatile and handy in the lower grades, because children don't have to be grouped to use them. I begin teaching watercolor techniques at the second grade level. By then most kids have the manual skills needed to control them. Order watercolor sets, one for each child, or add them to the list of school supplies you want your class to bring. Soup cans make the best water containers. Each child should bring one to be stored in a box on a shelf until needed. Before a painting session, fill the cans; then distribute them. Obtain a large plastic bucket (janitorial cleaning liquids come in nice-sized containers with handles). At the end of the lesson, place the bucket and the storage box next to the door. Before children leave to wash their hands, they should empty their water cans into the bucket and put the cans in the box.

CLEANING WATERCOLORS

Before doing any watercolor work, teach your students how to care for them. New sets are so pretty and clean that children often fret when they become "used" looking. The box is going to get dirty, but as long as the paints themselves are reasonably clean, they needn't worry. A good rule to follow is to mix only two colors at a time. It is foolish to mix all eight colors together. You end up with "mud." To clean a paint pan, rinse the brush and wipe the paint. Rinse and repeat until the paint is clean. Never hold the paint set under a faucet. You'll wash a lot of good paint down the drain. If, at the end of a painting session, the paints are puddly, blot them with a paper towel. Wipe excess water out of the paint box. Well-cared-for water-colors will last several years. One more thing, I have a preference for the Prang brand. They are more expensive than some, but they last longer and the colors are brighter.

SO WHO CARES IF THE BOX GETS DIRTY, AS LONG AS THE PAINTS ARE CLEAN.

WET-ON-WET WATERCOLORS

2nd-3rd Grades

12″ x 18″ white or manilla drawing paper, table covers, water, watercolors

Try this for an introduction to watercolors. It's a bit messy, but children find it fascinating.

Begin by wetting the paper. Dip your hand into the water can, and smear the water around, being sure to cover the entire paper evenly. Tell the kids that their brushes should not touch their papers today. They should use very wet brushes and lots of paint. Begin with any color (avoid black), and holding the loaded brush over the paper, squeeze out a drop of paint.

Repeat. Drop the color randomly over the paper until you have several splotches. Switch to a new color and repeat the process. Continue until the paper is filled with color. The colors will blend and mix on their own. Remember, don't touch the brush to the paper! Remind the children to work to the edges of the page. If puddles develop, blot them with a paper towel.

FOLLOW-UP

The colors and shapes in the paintings may suggest subject matter—bouquets of flowers, butterflies, balloons, the circus. While the papers are still wet, the children can draw on them with pastels. They should be careful not to cover too much of the paint. Some may want to make something out of the shapes of the paint splotches while others will use the colors as a background.

Use dry papers in the same manner. When the paper is dry you have more options. Crayons, pastels, or cut paper can be added to the colors to make a finished picture.

CRAYON RESIST

2nd-3rd Grades

12″ x 18″ white drawing or manilla paper, crayons, watercolors, water, table covers

STREAKS of BLUE, BLACK and PURPLE TURN DAY into SPOOKY HALLOWEEN NIGHT!

STAR WARS! FLUORESCENT CRAYONS ARE EFFECTIVE HERE!

Precede this lesson with a demonstration of the entire process. An important factor here is the HEAVY application of crayon. Ask the kids if they know what crayons are made of. What happens when water lands on wax? Does it soak in? No, the wax keeps out or "resists" the water. That's the basis of this technique.

Tape a paper to the chalkboard. Make several patches of different colors with the crayons. Include white, even though it won't show well at first. Color a couple of patches very lightly to show what will happen if the crayon isn't applied heavily enough. For a dramatic demonstration, use black paint. While the crayon needs a heavy hand, the paint should be applied with a delicate touch. Use lots of water and lots of paint. Brush lightly over the crayon and watch it pop through the paint. (Some brands of paint will cover the crayon. Here again, Prange Watercolors work best. Children with other brands may want to do a test paper.)

This technique is well-suited to a number of themes. See the illustrations for ideas.

CRAYON DESIGNS ON LARGE EGG SHAPE

···· PAINT ALL ONE COLOR OR DIFFERENT COLORS.

FOR WATERY EFFECT, WET PAPER, THEN STREAK BLUE, GREEN, PERHAPS PURPLE and BLACK PAINT OVER CRAYONED SEA LIFE.

PAINTING WITH TEMPERA

I know what you're thinking. PAINTING? Too messy, too difficult, too much trouble. What if somebody SPILLS something? You have a point, but what are the priorities here? Children need to paint. It's an important visual medium. It is fluid. A brush acts differently than a pencil or crayon. Painting is one of the best ways to learn about colors and how they react to each other. Above all, children get a feeling of satisfaction from pushing wet paint around on the paper. Have you ever watched the faces of kids who are caught up in painting? So, yes, you will have to risk a spill and summon a little extra energy on painting days, but you will do it because you are a good teacher, and you want the best for your students.

Getting the materials organized is half the battle. If your budget allows for a set of paints for each child, that's great. Most budgets are limited, forcing imaginative solutions to the problem of sharing paint. After years of experimenting, I've settled on using plastic cups with lids for paint containers. These are kept in muffin pans, which are easy to carry and store, as they can be stacked. I buy gallon jugs of the primary and secondary colors, black and white, which I use to refill the cups. I also mix six or eight special colors (pink, lavender, pine green, light blue, red-brown). These are used as needed by individuals who take them from a supply cart and return them when they are finished. Special colors are not always made available. The school cafeteria supplies the gallon cans for water. Children group their

desks in fours and each child is assigned a number, one through four. Materials are distributed by numbers. For instance, one's pass out paper, then sit down. Two's get water cans, and so on. It's best to explain the lesson before handing out brushes. When it's time to clean up, assign jobs again. As the children complete their assignments, they may leave to wash their hands.

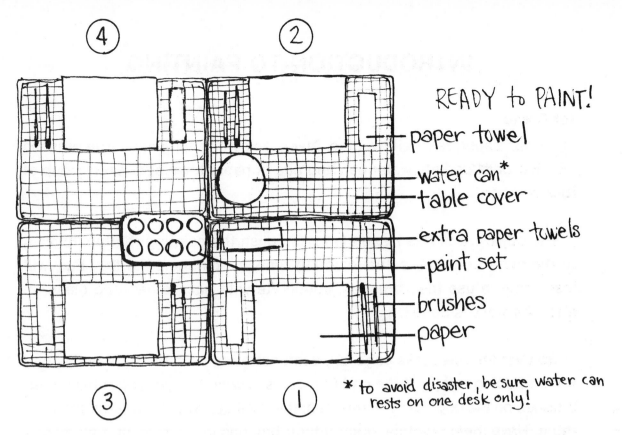

As in any other activity, when planning a painting project, know what it is you want the children to learn. Set up problems for them to solve, like how can you make a painting with nothing but seven different shades of green? In March the leprechauns play tricks with the paint, and you teach your students about monochromatic color schemes.

Get ready! Get set! PAINT!

59

INTRODUCTION TO PAINTING

1st Grade

12″ x 18″ paper; red, yellow, blue, black, and white tempera; large brushes (½″ flat or #12 point); water can and pile of paper towels for each group of four children

The objective of this lesson is to establish the painting routine. Explain to the class that their actual painting time will be short but that they will learn how to use their brushes, cooperate with each other, and clean up after the work is done.

Go over the rules (see page 15), demonstrating both the right and wrong ways of doing things. If the children can see why they shouldn't bang their brushes on the edge of the water can, they will be more likely to do the right thing. Have them practice dipping their brushes into the paint, rinsing correctly, and blotting.

This is one of the few times when no theme is given. Ask the class for ideas for paintings. You'll get plenty of responses. Tell the children that when they have an idea, they may begin. Someone is bound to complain because there is no green. Discourage mixing colors. (That's another lesson!) Suggest that a different color be substituted.

Allow plenty of time for cleanup. It's best to do one job at a time. If you start by collecting the brushes, that forces everyone to stop painting. Proceed to gather water cans, paints, and newspapers. The children should help with all of this, of course. Have a cleanup crew wipe desks, chairs, and floor with damp towels, while the others wash their hands. Find a corner of the room where the wet paintings can be spread out to dry. Try to use the same location each time you paint. After a time or two, the children will automatically put their paintings there.

PATTERNS IN PAINT

1st-2nd-3rd Grades

12″ x 18″ drawing or colored construction paper; large brushes (½″ flat or #12 point), small (#6 or #7 watercolor) brushes; set of paints including the primary and secondary colors, black, and white; water can; and paper towels for each group of four

Instruct children to think of the first letter of their first name and to paint it on the left side of the paper in any color. It should touch the top, left side, and bottom of the page. Demonstrate with your own initial. When everyone has done this, have them paint the first letter of their middle name. Demonstrate; then, the first letter of their last name. Demonstrate. The letters should touch the edges of the paper and each other. They can be all the same color or not.

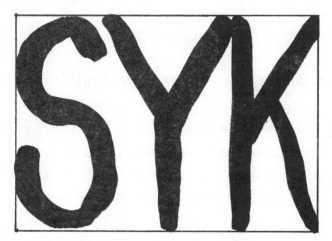

At this point, all brushes go into the water cans and stay there until after the following discussion. Ask the class to define the word *pattern*. Guide the discussion until it is clear that the meaning they will be using for this lesson is the repetition of a figure, shape, or line. Compare patterns to solids. Name various patterns— polka-dots, checks, stripes, florals. Have people who are wearing these patterns stand. If you have access to them, show the class reproductions or slides of famous paintings which include patterns. The work of Henri Matisse would be good.

Tell the children that by painting their initials, they have divided the paper into interesting spaces. Now they are to paint a pattern in each space, until the paper is completely filled.

Here are some hints:

1) It is okay to paint a space a solid color, let it dry, then paint stripes or dots on top. Demonstrate.

2) Another way to paint stripes is to paint all of one color, leaving spaces open; then fill in the spaces with another color. This saves much brush washing. Demonstrate.

3) It is not only okay but a good idea to use the same pattern more than once or vary a pattern by using different colors or sizes.

4) Painting light colors next to dark colors helps all colors show better.

5) Use the big brush for large spaces and the little brush for details.

A few children will say they are done when there is still space to fill. Encourage them to keep going. Some will not have time to finish. Before cleanup, announce that all papers are acceptable, even if a few empty spaces are left. The important thing is that all are now paying attention to the patterns around them.

If you want to go the extra mile, hang the paintings up along with three or four examples of patterns—perhaps a reproduction of a Matisse painting, a swatch of fabric, and a piece of patterned wallpaper.

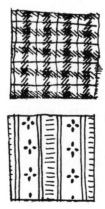

ODALISQUE by HENRI MATISSE

GRYPHONS AND OTHER BEASTS

3rd Grade

18″ x 24″ newsprint, tempera (primaries, secondaries, black, white, and a few special mixes), brushes (#6 or #7 watercolor and a larger size), water, paper towels, desk covers

Prepare students for this lesson by giving them time to experiment with their brushes. Use black paint and as much paper as you need—that's the reason for newsprint. It's cheap, and the kids will go through lots of it.

THIN LINES • THICK LINES • CURVES • WIGGLES • THIN to THICK and VICE VERSA

Demonstrate strokes they should try. After 15-20 minutes, gather everyone together in a circle on the floor to talk about mythical beasts, their history and importance. Show examples of various interpretations of the gryphon. Have the children locate the lion parts and eagle parts. *Cricket Magazine*, November 1984, has an excellent article on gryphons.

Have the children go back to work. Each should draw an historical mythical beast or one of his own design. He should use a brush and black paint to complete the line drawing. Color will come at a later time. The student should try to fill the page. Allow him to start over if he needs to, but ask that everyone have a drawing by the end of the class period. If a child with a good drawing makes a minor mistake, glue a newsprint patch over the goof, and tell him to continue working. Let the drawings dry. Plan to allow two more sessions for painting the beasts.

Since the paper is so large, the kids won't have room on their desks for large water cans and paint sets. You can get around this by having them use the soup cans they have brought with their watercolors (see page 55). Put all of the paints on a table and have each student take one color at a time to his seat or place on the floor. There will be a lot of moving around, so caution everyone that you will not stand for any nonsense. As a child finishes with a color, he should return it to the supply table and get another color. Show the class the special mixes that are available.

Before painting begins, talk about color. Some suggestions:

1) Put light colors next to dark colors, dull next to bright, for contrast.

2) Repeat a color in different parts of the painting. The repetition helps keep the viewer's eyes circulating on the paper.

3) Think about a limited palette, that is, using only 3 or 4 colors and no more.

4) Don't forget to consider the background. It's part of the painting, too.

As they are working, circulate and give encouragement. I think you will see the students become totally involved in their paintings. When they ask your opinion or advice, don't answer too quickly. Many times while you are "thinking," they will come up with their own solutions. Throughout the activity, remind the kids to watch their step, and keep a large supply of paper towels on hand for the inevitable spills.

When it is all done, you will find that the beast has brought out the best in your students.

CUT-PAPER PROJECTS

When you draw, the marks stay where you put them. Cut and paste projects present children with another way of thinking. Because a composition is built piece by piece, it is easy to shift elements around. It's important to let children take advantage of this. Don't allow them to glue until they have had time to experiment with different arrangements. Cut paper is the medium to use if you want your students to think "shape." It provides a balance for the linear thinking involved in drawing. Children need to be aware of both elements to master visual expression. Training in shape perception through cut paper helps a child to see how the shapes of the parts combine to make the whole. We can then link shape to drawing. Drawing many simple parts is much less threatening than trying to draw a complex image all at once. When doing cut paper, encourage the kids to imagine the shapes in their minds; then cut directly into the paper without drawing first. Almost anything can be broken down into circles, squares, triangles, and rectangles. In this section you will find several projects. Some deal specifically with shape and others explore paper which is folded and cut.

SHAPE

1st-2nd Grades

construction paper: 12″ x 18″ black, 6″ x 9″ red, yellow, and blue; glue; scissors; paper towels for wiping off excess glue

The motivation for this activity might be one of the many books about shape which are available in children's book stores and libraries.* If you can't locate a book, begin the lesson with a discussion of the four basic shapes—triangle, rectangle, square, and circle. Ask the children to name the shapes as you list and draw them on the chalkboard.

Have the class move to another part of the room and sit in a circle on the floor. Place a sheet of the black construction paper in the middle of the circle, along with a collection of the four shapes, precut in a variety of sizes and all three primary colors. (The children should leave their own papers at their seats.) The following "play" period helps make the object of the lesson clear, that only the four basic shapes may be cut; they can then be put together to make a picture of something.

Place a red, yellow, or blue rectangle lengthwise on the black paper. Point out the top of the paper. Tell the class that the rectangle represents a person's body. Ask if someone can add one shape to begin to complete the person. The children will be eager to help. Let them take turns adding parts until the person is fairly complete. Carefully remove the rectangular body and replace it with a triangle. See how the person looks more like a girl now?

*I like to use *Squares Are Not Bad,* by Violet Salazar, Golden Press, 1967.

67

Dump all the shapes on the floor and try the whole building process once more. Make something different this time—a house, truck, rocket, train, flower. Before the children go back to their seats, tell them they must obey the rules of the game today. Have them rename the shapes they are allowed to cut. Only the four basic shapes are permitted. They can make whatever they choose as long as they follow the rules. Encourage them to think of something original. They should cut only what they need! In every class there are one or two who will spend the entire work time chopping up their papers into shapes with no idea of what they're going to do with them. Review gluing techniques, and let work begin. Talk with individual children as they are working, giving extra help to those who need it. Encourage filling the paper, careful gluing, and cutting through several layers of paper at once if more than one of something is needed.

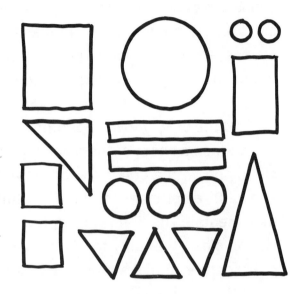

Don't be surprised at the range of ideas and abilities. Some children will copy the demonstration pictures, some will make several unrelated images, some will show unusual skill in cutting and composing, and finally there will be a few whose papers resemble the inside of a wastebasket.

COLORS LOOK BRIGHTER on BLACK!

68

SNOWFLAKES

1st Grade

colored tissue paper, 4½ " x 6"; cardboard circles, 3" and 4" in diameter; 9" x 12" white drawing paper; scissors; rubber cement

Everybody knows how to make paper snowflakes, right? Wrong. Somewhere along the line we were taught. First graders, whatever their snowflakes experience, are always fascinated by the surprise element in cutting folded paper. Although real snowflakes are six-sided, it's easier for young children to fold an eight-sided flake. Let everyone choose three colors of tissue paper. Tell the class that tissue paper is transparent. Write the word on the board. Ask them if they can see how tissue paper is different from other kinds of paper. Keep taking ideas until someone says that you can see through it. Have them overlap two of their colors and hold them up to the light to see what new color is formed. Give each child a large and small cardboard circle pattern. Have them draw around the patterns and cut out circles. When everyone has at least one circle cut, have them work along with you to fold and cut the first snowflake. The folding is easier if you make the following comparisons:

TACO

FAN

ICE-CREAM CONE

1) Fold the circle in half to make a "taco."

2) Fold in half again to make a "fan."

3) Fold in half once more to make an "ice-cream cone." After the first time, if they forget, just tell them "taco, fan, ice-cream cone." and they'll be on their way.

There are three "for sure" places to cut and one "maybe." Paper should not be unfolded until shapes have been cut out of both sides and the top of the ice-cream cone. The kids can cut more than one hole in a side, but caution them to leave a little paper between holes and not to cut clear to the point of the cone. If they want a hole in the center of the snowflake, they should cut off the tip of the cone. Now open!

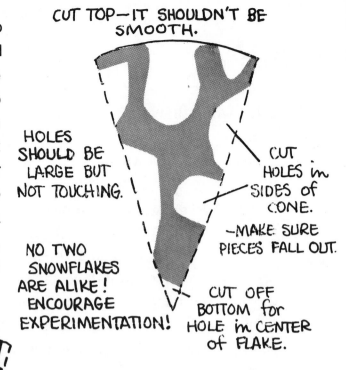

CUT TOP—IT SHOULDN'T BE SMOOTH.

HOLES SHOULD BE LARGE BUT NOT TOUCHING.

CUT HOLES in SIDES of CONE.

—MAKE SURE PIECES FALL OUT.

NO TWO SNOWFLAKES ARE ALIKE! ENCOURAGE EXPERIMENTATION!

CUT OFF BOTTOM for HOLE in CENTER of FLAKE.

TRY THESE CUTS for DIFFERENT SHAPES (PLUS HOLES in SIDES, OF COURSE!).

Tell the children they will arrange their snowflakes on the white paper. They should overlap the flakes a bit. Snow doesn't fall in straight, orderly lines, does it? Besides, overlapping will take advantage of the transparency of the colors. To keep from tearing the tissue paper, paint a circle of rubber cement on the white paper; then lay the snowflake in it. If they have time, students can get more tissue. Some children may make as many as ten snowflakes.

Don't let the idea of colored snow bother you. These snowflakes fell right through a rainbow!

VALENTINE COLLAGE

1st-2nd-3rd Grades

9″ x 12″ oaktag; 9″ x 12″, 6″ x 9″, and 4½″ x 6″ construction paper in a variety of colors; other kinds of paper, such as wallpaper, foil, tissue, and gift wrap; yarn; large needles; scissors; paper punches; glue; ribbon; lace; rickrack; fabric scraps; flower catalogues; paper doilies; heart stickers

Several days preceding this activity, ask your students to look for some of the items listed above and bring them to school. They should not go out and buy lots of "stuff" but bring things they have on hand. Of course, you will have to have plenty for those who bring nothing. (If you have a phobia about glitter, as I do, specify that no glitter be brought.)

The motivation for making valentines is present. You don't have to get the children "up" for this activity. You should, however, spend some time getting them to think about what they want to do and for whom their valentines are intended. Give everyone a piece of oaktag. The heavier paper makes a sturdy background for collage. Demonstrate how to fold and cut a heart; then discuss briefly each of the following ideas.

1) What shape will the valentine be? Will you leave the paper rectangular or cut it into a heart?

2) How will you use the materials you brought? Do you want to glue lace all around the edge of your valentine? Do you want to stitch on it? Or punch holes to lace ribbon through?

3) If you plan to glue several hearts on top of one another, it is best to begin with the smallest first. Use the first one as a pattern for the next, cutting it slightly larger. This way all the hearts will be about the same shape.

4) Why not experiment with color? How about a valentine all in shades of blue or brown? What about black, red, and gold or navy, pink, and lace?

5) If your valentine is to be rectangular, how will you arrange it? Something big in the middle, with smaller decorations in the corners? Borders? An informal arrangement?

6) Maybe you could put a heart on a spring so it will pop out. Can you use the scrap that's left after you cut out a heart—the negative space?

With these thoughts in mind, let the work begin. Be on hand to help with punching, stitching and advice. You'll enjoy the total involvement of this project. The children will feel a real sense of satisfaction at having experienced valentines the old-fashioned way. They mean so much more when they have the personal touch.

JUNGLE COLLAGE

1st-2nd Grades

12″ x 18″ light blue or gray construction paper; 6″ x 9″ construction paper in gray, orange, yellow, brown, light green, green, dark green, black, and white; 2″ x 18″ and 3″ x 18″ strips in shades of green; scrap paper; glue; scissors; crayons; two or three examples of jungle scenes by Henri Rousseau (look in comprehensive art history books, late nineteenth century); pictures of jungle plants and animals

This activity can be organized into three parts: background trees, animals, and jungle grasses and plants. It will take more than one session to complete. The motivation comes from the Rousseau pictures. Tell the students a little bit about the artist. He was French and worked as a customs officer until he was forty. When he quit his job to be a painter, his friends thought he was foolish. He didn't have any art training. He visited botanical gardens and zoos to get ideas for his paintings. He never saw a jungle.

Ask the students if they know what *overlap* means. See if they can point to places in Rousseau's paintings where he has shown one thing behind another. Overlapping parts in a picture helps an artist show near and far space. If we were going to build a jungle scene from cut paper, would we want to begin with the parts that are farthest away or closest? It makes sense to begin with the background and work forward. We will do trees first to create a jungle atmosphere. What kinds of trees grow in tropical climates? Have you ever seen palm trees? The leaves form a kind of umbrella over the trunk.

Demonstrate for the class how to tear green leafy shapes. Ask the kids to glue five or six trees to the background paper. They may glue the trunks, then cut or tear big leaves. The tops of the trees should reach almost to the top of the paper. The trunks may or may not touch the bottom. For the sake of good design, the trees should have some variety. One may be very tall, one may bend to the left or right. Different shades of green paper should be used for the leaves.

Animals can be cut in pieces and assembled with glue, using the appropriate color of 6″ x 9″ paper. Some children may prefer to draw the entire animal and cut it out. Whichever method is used, take a few minutes to look at pictures of animals and notice the simple shapes that make up heads, bodies, legs, ears. The elephant has a round head and body, triangular ears, snake-like trunk. The rhino has a body like a kidney bean. The giraffe's body is rectangular, its legs and neck are long and thin, its head, is triangular. The animals should not be glued to the background until some jungle plants and grasses have been cut out. Students should experiment with overlapping animals, plants, and trees, so that the animals appear to be strolling through the foliage.

Use the long strips of green to cut grasses and plants. To make quick work out of a stretch of grass, fold a strip in half twice. Cut zigzags from fold to fold and open. Both halves of the paper can be used. Encourage the kids to use more than one shade of green. For plants, use a piece of a strip. Fold it in half and cut zigzags as shown in the diagram. Use bright colors from the scrap box to add tropical fruits or flowers.

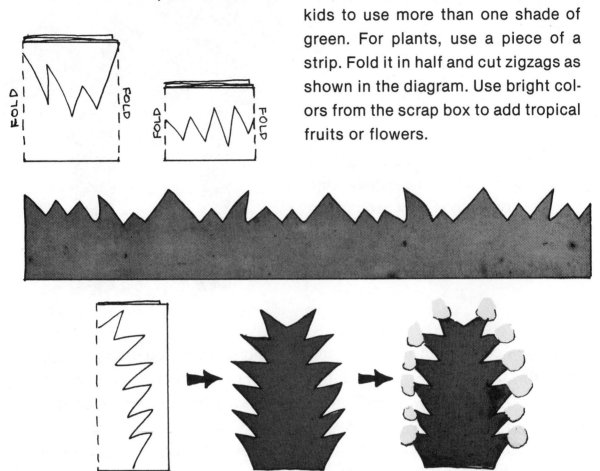

Arrange plants and animals; then glue. If a tree is needed in the foreground, add it. Use crayons for filling in "holes" in the jungle, animal spots and features, outlining . . .

Hang the pictures side by side across the room to create one long jungle frieze.

INSECTS

1st-2nd Grades

12″ x 18″ construction paper in assorted colors, 6″ x 9″ construction paper in assorted colors, pictures of insects (ant, fly, bee, dragonfly, and others), scissors, glue

Tape pictures of insects to the chalkboard. If you are using pictures in books, gather the class around you, with the books on a table or the floor where everyone can see. Explain to the children that scientists group things that have like characteristics. Ask them to look at the insects to discover what features they have alike. Make a list as they tell you what they

see. All insects have: eyes, legs—how many? six, antennae, wings (all but the ant), hair (yes, they do!). Draw attention to the main body parts. All insects have a head, thorax, and abdomen. People have heads and abdomens, too. Where are the wings and legs joined to an insect? To the thorax. Notice the segmented tails.

Let everyone choose a large piece of paper for a background and three small ones to use for an insect. The rules are that everybody must use cut paper only (no crayon today), and start with a head, thorax, and abdomen or three main body parts. These parts can be the same or different colors. They should be fairly large. Demonstrate. After the main parts are glued down, each student is free to use his imagination. An insect may have seventeen legs if the artist so desires.

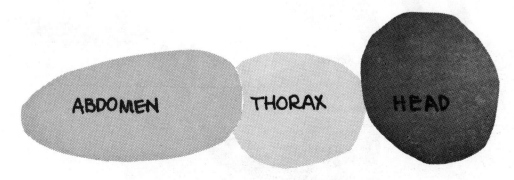

THREE MAIN PARTS

Encourage the kids to use stripes and spots on different parts of the insect to add color and interest.

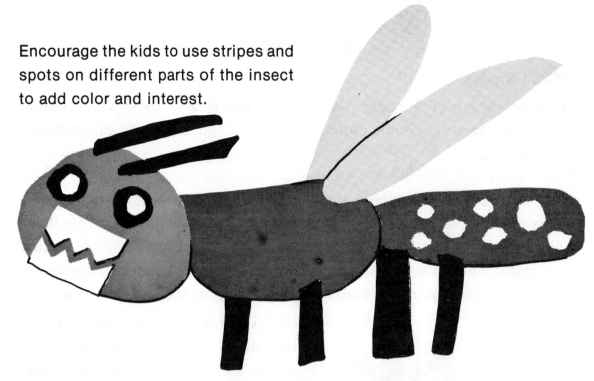

As the class works, circulate, offering suggestions and help. When you see that the insects are nearing completion, tell the students to add some background details to show where the insect is—a flower, some blades of grass, a leaf, a tree branch, the sun, some clouds.

Tape a fly swatter on the wall next to the insect pictures, but don't let anybody use it!

CUT-PAPER TOTEMS

2nd-3rd Grades

9″ x 12″ construction paper in a variety of bright colors and black, scrap box or scrap paper left over from other projects, scissors, glue, pictures of authentic Northwest Indian totem poles and masks (you can find these in books). If you have a source of films, get *The Loon's Necklace.* It is an excellent motivator for this project.

Show the class several examples of masks by the Indian tribes of the Northwest. Draw attention to features which have been designed or "stylized." Eyes and mouths will show similarities from mask to mask. Talk about what the different masks represent—animals, sun, moon, medicine man. Note the shapes of the masks. Many of them are "symmetrical."

Explain and demonstrate how a symmetrical shape can be cut by folding the paper in half first. Draw two or three possible variations on the board, but make it clear that these are only suggestions. Encourage the students to experiment with their own shapes. They may want to draw a line on the paper and have you check it before they cut. (This will save lots of paper!) Go over the explanations given below for paper sculpture techniques. Again, a diagram on the board would be useful.

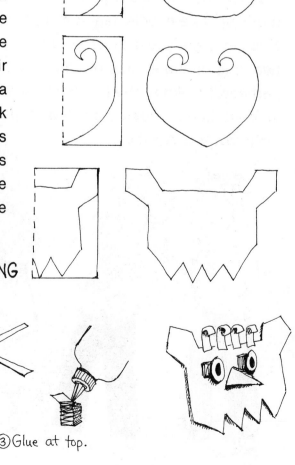

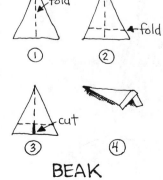

BEAK

CAT STAIR SPRING

① Glue 2 strips of paper together as shown.

② Fold one strip over the other until the paper runs out.

③ Glue at top.

79

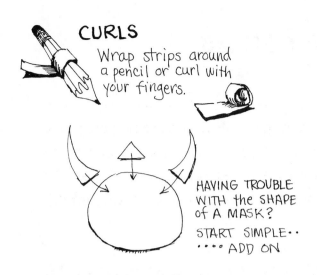

CURLS

Wrap strips around a pencil or curl with your fingers.

HAVING TROUBLE WITH the SHAPE of A MASK?

START SIMPLE·· ····° ADD ON

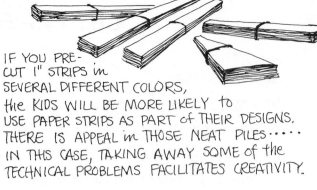

IF YOU PRE- CUT 1" STRIPS in SEVERAL DIFFERENT COLORS, the KIDS WILL BE MORE LIKELY to USE PAPER STRIPS AS PART of THEIR DESIGNS. THERE IS APPEAL in THOSE NEAT PILES····· IN THIS CASE, TAKING AWAY SOME of the TECHNICAL PROBLEMS FACILITATES CREATIVITY.

Let each child select a sheet of paper for the mask along with several pieces of scrap paper. They should return for more scrap paper as needed. The most difficult thing for some students is cutting that shape on the fold. If someone is having great difficulty cutting around horns or ears, suggest that he cut a simpler shape; then add on the rest. While they are working, help with technical problems and encourage the kids to fill the space. Indian artists hate empty places!

When the masks are finished, tape them up totem pole fashion. If the class is large, you may need to make two, one on either side of your door, perhaps. You know the kid that needs an extra boost? Put his mask on top. He'll love you for that.

LETTERS

3rd Grade

2¼" x 3" construction paper in assorted colors—precut a pile of each color and bind with a rubber band until you're ready to use it—scissors, envelopes

Letter cutting is a skill that is useful throughout the school years. You may want to teach the technique without assigning a finished project. Get everyone started in a 20-30 minute session with the whole group. They could then work independently at a center. If you choose to have the students use their letters, allow 2-3 sessions to complete the projects.

Give everyone a pile of black paper to practice with. Tell the kids they will be thinking of capitals in the block letter style. This means that they won't cut curves. Looking at the rectangular paper, they must imagine a letter hiding there. All they need to do is cut away some of the paper to expose it. Begin with the letter "A." Demonstrate with 6" x 9" rectangles so the class can see what you are doing. To further clarify, draw diagrams on the board. An "A" is a house with a door and a window. Have everybody cut a door. Bury the scissors into the paper above the door and cut the window. A "B" is two windows. Demonstrate. If you want to indicate curves, cut a notch on the right side of the "B" between the windows. Clip the right-hand corners. Continue through

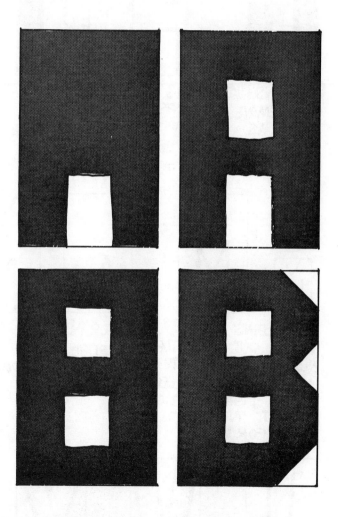

several more letters, allowing the students to request the ones they can't visualize. Refer to the diagrams. Save the practice letters in envelopes.

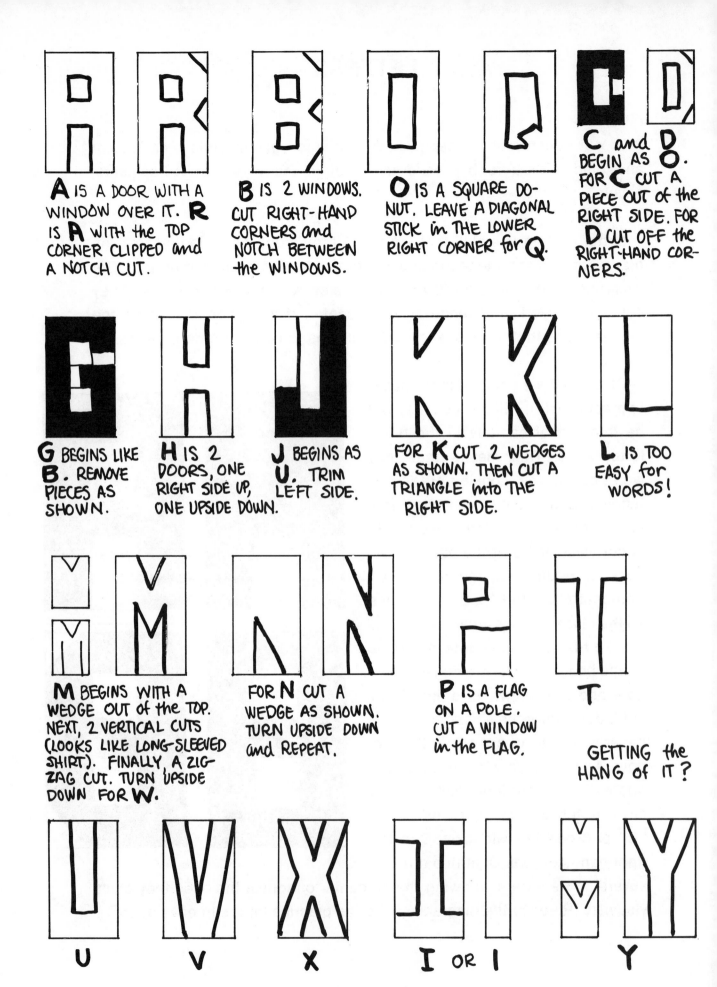

A IS A DOOR WITH A WINDOW OVER IT. **R** IS **A** WITH THE TOP CORNER CLIPPED and A NOTCH CUT.

B IS 2 WINDOWS. CUT RIGHT-HAND CORNERS and NOTCH BETWEEN the WINDOWS.

O IS A SQUARE DO-NUT. LEAVE A DIAGONAL STICK IN THE LOWER RIGHT CORNER for **Q**.

C and **D** BEGIN AS **O**. FOR **C** CUT A PIECE OUT of the RIGHT SIDE. FOR **D** CUT OFF the RIGHT-HAND COR-NERS.

G BEGINS LIKE **B**. REMOVE PIECES AS SHOWN.

H IS 2 DOORS, ONE RIGHT SIDE UP, ONE UPSIDE DOWN.

J BEGINS AS **U**. TRIM LEFT SIDE.

FOR **K** CUT 2 WEDGES AS SHOWN. THEN CUT A TRIANGLE into THE RIGHT SIDE.

L IS TOO EASY for WORDS!

M BEGINS WITH A WEDGE OUT of the TOP. NEXT, 2 VERTICAL CUTS (LOOKS LIKE LONG-SLEEVED SHIRT). FINALLY, A ZIG-ZAG CUT. TURN UPSIDE DOWN FOR **W**.

FOR **N** CUT A WEDGE AS SHOWN. TURN UPSIDE DOWN and REPEAT.

P IS A FLAG ON A POLE. CUT A WINDOW in the FLAG.

T

GETTING the HANG OF IT?

U

V

X

I OR **I**

Y

CUT THESE LETTERS SIDEWAYS····

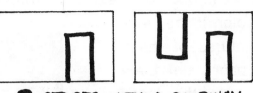

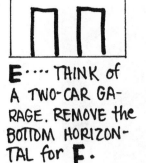

E···· THINK of A TWO-CAR GA-RAGE. REMOVE the BOTTOM HORIZON-TAL for **F**.

S STARTS WITH A DOORWAY ON the RIGHT. TURN UPSIDE DOWN and REPEAT.

Z IS CUT LIKE A SIDEWAYS **N**.

PROJECT IDEAS

letter-cutting paper in assorted colors, 12″ x 18″ construction paper in assorted colors, scissors, glue

Discuss maxims with your class. Read and list several on the board. Most third graders are unfamiliar with maxims and their meanings. If you want to have some fun, list only the first half of the maxims and let your students fill in their own endings. Have each child letter the maxim of his choice. He should cut all letters and arrange them on the paper before gluing. Discuss with him ways he might arrange the letters and words on the paper to make a pleasing and readable design.

Talk with the kids about what they want to be when they grow up. Have them letter their names in one color and their professions, following their names, in another color. If they like, they could draw pictures of themselves on drawing paper, cut them out, and glue them to the "me" posters. Again, there should be some thought given to the placement of the letters so that they are readable.

Combine the cut letters with crayon or marker and have children add lines to make pictures.

A "V" "T.P."

LETTERS CAN BE USED BACKWARDS UPSIDE DOWN OR SIDEWAYS.

THIS IS REALLY A "T" SHIRT!

Letter the alphabet. Make the letters different colors and different sizes.

ABCDEFGHIJKLMN
OPQRSTUVWXYZ

EMPHASIS ON DESIGN

By focusing on the elements of design, you can help your students become more adept at picture-making and more aware of natural and man-made designs in their environment. The emphasis in this section is on color, pattern, and arrangement.

DESIGNS SQUARED

3rd Grade

9″ x 9″ or 12″ x 12″ white drawing paper, 3″ x 3″ typing paper, felt-tipped markers in assorted colors, glue

This exercise has two parts. First the students will design one square; then, repeating the design eight (or eleven) more times, they will experiment with different arrangements. When they hit upon something they like, they will glue the nine (or twelve) small squares to the large square.

DESIGNING A SQUARE

Use markers to draw lines and shapes on one of the 3″ squares. Try to include the corners in the design. The first square becomes the pattern for the others. Place them one at a time over the pattern until you have nine or twelve matching squares.

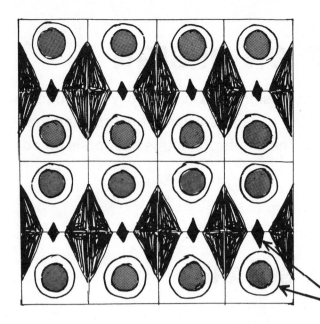

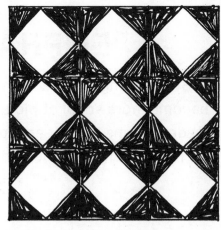

IT'S FASCINATING to SEE NEW SHAPES EMERGE AS YOU PUT the SQUARES TOGETHER·····ADDITIONS CAN BE MADE AFTER ALL the SQUARES ARE GLUED.

ARRANGING THE SQUARES

Arrange the squares three (four) across and three (four) down. Try turning them different ways and observe the patterns that are formed where squares come together. Be sure to allow sufficient "play" time. Glue the most pleasing arrangement to the large square.

Trim the finished designs to eliminate ragged edges. Mount them on construction paper, matching a color in the design. In evaluating the project, discuss how this type of design might be used. The children are sure to see the resemblance between their efforts and wallpaper, fabric, and flooring patterns.

FOR THIS PATTERN, 6 SQUARES ARE LIKE THIS············

······AND 3 SQUARES, LIKE THIS....

RADIAL DESIGN, SNOWFLAKES

2nd-3rd Grades

12" x 18" white drawing paper; felt-tipped markers in fine and regular points, assorted colors

Begin by having the class practice making six-armed stars on scrap paper. Tell the kids to think of cutting pie. All the slices should be the same size. After two or three minutes, let the children help you create a sample design. On a piece of paper taped to the board, draw the "skeleton" of the snowflake. Lines and shapes may be drawn between or on the original lines, but each addition must be done six times. Demonstrate. Now ask for a volunteer to add something else. Let two or three children make additions to the sample; then remove it and let everyone begin on his own design.

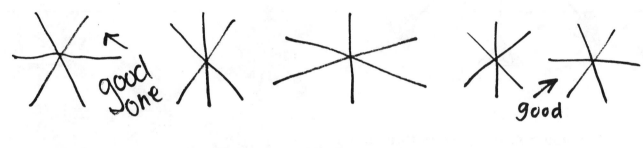

HINTS

1) Always work from the center out.

2) Let the design grow little by little, not by giant leaps.

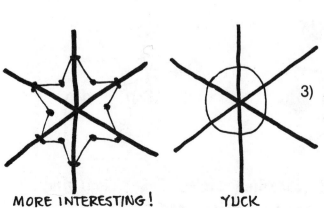

3) Avoid connecting the six points in a circle—BOR-ING!

MORE INTERESTING!   YUCK

4) Extend the arms of the skeleton if you want to add more to it.

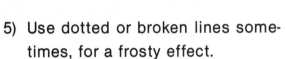

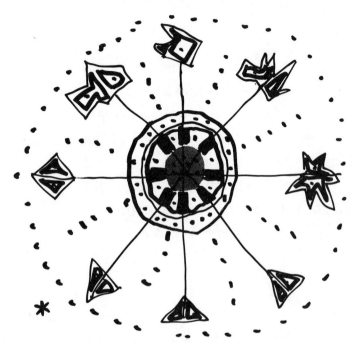

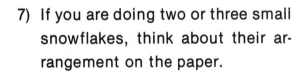

5) Use dotted or broken lines sometimes, for a frosty effect.

6) Try a limited color scheme.

7) If you are doing two or three small snowflakes, think about their arrangement on the paper.

Crop the finished designs and mount them on colored construction paper for display.

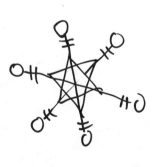

*This example has 8 "arms" and connecting circles. That's okay, and typical····· expect variations on your guidelines.

RADIAL DESIGN, A GAME

1st-2nd-3rd Grades

drawing paper, any size; crayons or markers

This game can be played by two or more players. It's a fun activity for those who have finished other work and have some time to spare.

Fold the paper in half both ways to find the center. One player draws a simple shape in the middle. The next adds to it, building on the fold lines or between them. The design grows until everybody involved in its creation decides that it is finished. Draw straws to see who gets to keep it!

WE DID IT!

SYMMETRICAL DESIGN, INDIAN STYLE

2nd-3rd Grades

12″ x 18″ white drawing paper, black tempera paint, watercolor brushes (#6 or #7), water, table covers, paper towels, pictures of Indian masks (look in books about Indians of the Northwest)

There are many approaches to mask-making. This one affords a graphic demonstration of the concept of symmetry. Arriving at symmetrical shapes in the way described below is less mysterious than the fold-and-cut method used in the Cut-Paper Totems project (page 79).

Gather the class around to look at pictures of Indian masks, or use an opaque projector to enlarge the pictures on the wall. Call attention to the matching features on each mask. Explain the word *symmetry*. Ask the children to tell you which parts of the masks are symmetrical and which are not. Many are totally symmetrical. Observe the shapes the Indians use for facial features, ears, horns. Now, to work!

Have everyone fold the paper in half shortwise. Open. Demonstrate the procedure for designing a symmetrical mask. Begin with the shape of the mask. Using black paint, draw a line which begins and ends on the fold. The

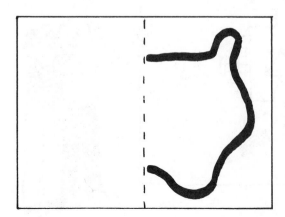
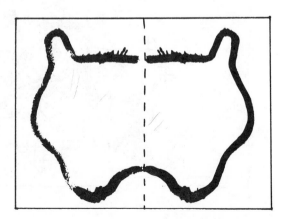

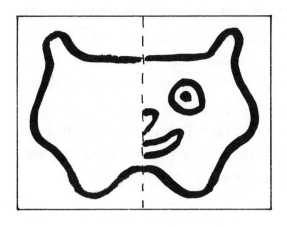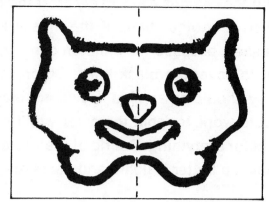

line should extend to within an inch or two of the edge of the paper at the top, side, and bottom. While the paint is wet, fold and blot the line onto the other half of the paper. Open. Ask for a student volunteer to draw an eye shape. Fold and blot. Since drawing the complete nose and mouth would result in two noses and two mouths after blotting, begin and end these features on the fold line as you did for the outline of the mask. Further, break up the spaces in the mask by drawing more shapes and lines. These may or may not be symmetrical. Break up the background space in the same way. The Indians do not like empty spaces in their designs. Remove the sample before letting the class begin.

Put the designs away to dry after the black line drawings are finished. Add color at another time. If the masks are to be painted, keep using small brushes, because the children can control the paint better and won't be so apt to cover the black lines. Oil crayons could be used as an alternative. They should be applied heavily for maximum color. The kids' own crayons would work, too, but the color won't be as vibrant. Encourage the children to color everything. Get rid of the white! Remind them that all the colors will show up better if lights and darks are placed next to each other.

Review the meaning of *symmetry* from time to time. The kids may forget the word, but they'll never forget how they made those masks!

SADIE AND DAN FROM PATTERNLAND

1st Grade

12″ x 18″ white drawing paper, felt-tipped markers in assorted colors and point sizes

Children have no problem understanding patterns. They can draw stripes, polka-dots, zigzags, checks. Ask them to fill a paper with patterns, and they'll do it. Why, then, in their drawings, are patterns seldom present? Perhaps it's easier to color solid colors. With the proper motivation couldn't we get our students to liven up their images with pattern? This lesson is designed to do just that.

Tell the class to listen carefully as you read them "Sadie-Sadie, the Pattern Lady."

Sadie-Sadie, the pattern lady,
Is the prettiest lady in town.
She ties ribbons fair in her patterned hair,
And has flowers all over her gown.
She takes her socks from a polka-dot box;
She puts them on pretty plaid feet.
Her beautiful shoes are a number of hues
That flash as she walks down the street.
Her favorite bonnet has feathers upon it
And sashes that tie 'neath her chin.
Her apron is darted and multiple-hearted;
It fastens in back with a pin.
And when people meet her, they happily greet her.
She glows from her toes to her crown.
Yes, Sadie-Sadie, the pattern lady,
Is the prettiest lady in town.

Explain any words the children might not have understood, then quiz them. What did Sadie wear in her hair? What did her apron have on it? Where did she keep her socks? And so on. Read "Dashing Dan, the Pattern Man." Again ask for careful listening.

Dashing Dan is a pattern man.
He comes from a place called Patternland.
He wears a checked coat and a tall striped hat
When he goes for a stroll with his calico cat.
His pants, a spectacular sight to behold,
Are covered with patterns of purple and gold.
A bright, shiny buckle on each shiny boot
Reflects the designs of his big bumbershoot.
His favorite tie was a gift from his mother.
It's dotted and spotted unlike any other.
And the colorful garment that covers his chest
Is a beautiful, sparkling, polka-dot vest.
So if you fancy colors of pink, green and blue,
I'll tell you a secret, between me and you,
That Dashing Dan is the handsomest man
Who lives in the village of Patternland.

Again, explain any difficult words; then quiz the students. They are to draw Sadie or Dan, but they need not draw them exactly as they were described. The important thing is to use lots of patterns. Some children may want to draw both characters. Encourage them to work big. Begin with a grapefruit-sized head so that the feet will reach the bottom of the paper. As the children draw, comment on their work. "I see Joey has drawn Dan's umbrella. Good job, Sara! Sadie's bonnet is beautiful." Your remarks will keep everyone thinking. Encourage the kids to draw ground, sky, trees and flowers along with the figures. Remind them that these things might look different in "Patternland." Toward the end of the period, read the poems once more to inspire last-minute additions.

different in "Patternland." Toward the end of the period, read the poems once more to inspire last-minute additions.

These pictures will no doubt be a bit extreme, but Sadie and Dan have taught a valuable lesson. Use them as a reference for future pictures when patterns are desirable.

* Probably due to the emphasis on pattern, this child forgot to draw arms!

KITES

1st-2nd Grades

12″ x 18″ white drawing paper; table covers; tempera paints in assorted colors; paper towels; pencil; straight edge; scissors; yarn in 12″ lengths; tissue paper in assorted colors, approximately 3″ x 4″; glue

Organization is the key to finishing this project in one sitting. Put the yarn, tissue paper and several bottles of glue on a table. This is the "tail table." Set the classroom up for painting. Help the children make a kite shape out of their papers. Tell them to fold the paper in half lengthwise. Unfold. Now fold it NOT QUITE IN HALF shortwise. Open. Make dots at the ends of the folds. Use a straight edge (a 2″ x 18″ strip of cardboard will work) to connect the dots. Cut on the lines. Some children will need help with all aspects of this procedure.

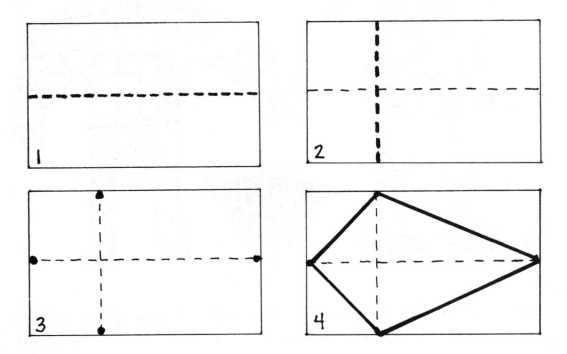

Have the children look at the shape before them. Can they tell which end is up? Remind them that when they begin designing, the long point goes at the bottom. Ask for ideas. What kind of design would look good on a kite? Allow time for different possibilities to come out. About this time someone will ask if the kites will really fly. They will only fly on the wall. They will decorate the room (hall), so make them pretty!

When a student finishes painting his kite, he may go to the tail table. The kite should be left on his desk to dry. Show the class how to make bows by pinching or twisting the tissue paper pieces in the middle. Use a drop of glue to stick the bow to the yarn. Encourage the kids to think about the colors and arrangement of the bows. Some children will select all one color tissue paper, some will alternate two or three colors, and some will take one of each. After the bows are glued in place, put a dot of glue on the end of the yarn. Go back and glue it to the kite, which should be about dry.

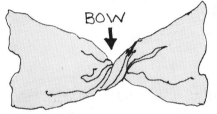

BOW

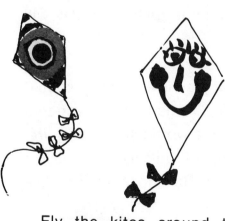

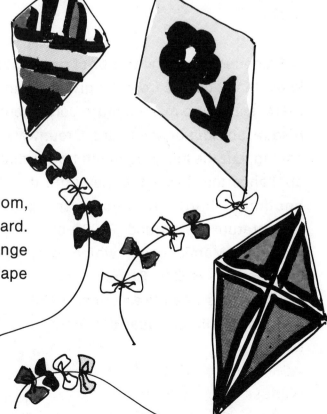

Fly the kites around the room, down the hall, or on a bulletin board. To make them look natural, arrange them at different heights, and tape the tails into windswept curves.

CLAY

Children love to work with clay. In informal polls taken at year's end, clay always heads the list of favorite media. If you have access to a kiln, plan to fire and glaze the pottery your students make. Clay sculpture can be fired once, then painted. If there is no kiln available, use a commercial self-hardening clay. Aside from group projects, you might have a clay center, where children can explore the medium independently. Children from first grade on can master simple clay building techniques, beginning with pinch pots and working into slab construction and joining procedures.

PINCH POTS

1st Grade

clay, a ball the size of an orange for each child; clay tools or assorted plastic knives, forks, and spoons; Popsicle sticks; table covers (can be canvas or cut-up plastic tablecloths—should have some texture or clay will stick)

Precede the work with a brief discussion about clay. The children should know that it comes from the ground, that it is fragile when it dries, and that there is a way to make it more permanent. Write the words *greenware*, *fire*, *bisque*, and *kiln* on the board. Greenware is dried, unfired clay. Firing is like baking, but the kiln gets much hotter than an oven. The kiln is the oven-like appliance that heats the clay until it becomes hard. It heats to a temperature of around 2000° compared to Mom's oven, which only goes as high as 500°. Bisque refers to clay that has been fired once. Insist that the children use the correct terms.

THE TEACHER KILLED MY POT!

NO SHE DIDN'T, SILLY. SHE FIRED YOUR POT in the KILN.

Before handing out the clay, demonstrate the entire pinch pot procedure. Holding the ball of clay in your nonwriting hand, use the thumb of your other hand to push a hole into the ball. Push until you can feel the pressure of your thumb on your palm, but not hard enough to go clear through. Now, with thumb always on the inside and straight fingers on the outside, turn the ball around and around in your cupped palm, pinching as you turn. The hole will get bigger as the sides or "walls" of the pot become thinner. Strive for even thickness throughout, including the bottom. Keep in mind that pottery is not fine china. The walls of a pinch pot should be about ¼ " thick.

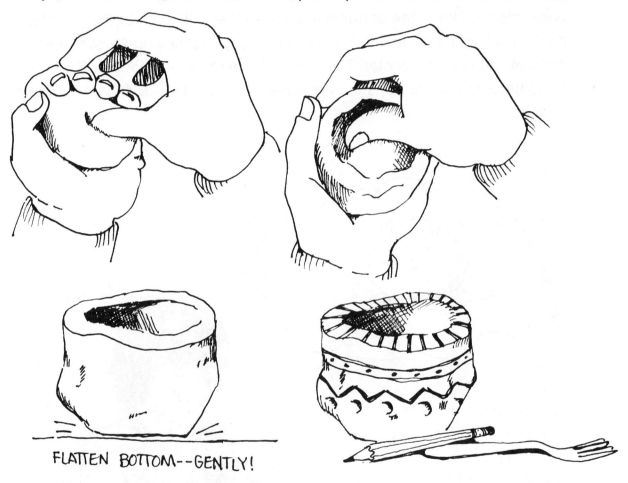

FLATTEN BOTTOM--GENTLY!

Caution the children not to put their pots down on the table while pinching or to get their fingers inside and thumb outside. Both practices can lead to collapsed or otherwise out-of-control pots. After the pot is satisfactorily formed, drop it GENTLY on the table three or four times to flatten the bottom. Tools can be used to add texture or decoration. Write each child's name and the year on the bottom of his pot before putting it away to dry. After several days, the pots will be dry enough to fire.

GLAZING

Glazing is a mysterious process that children have to take on faith until they have done it once. It is difficult for them to understand that the gray, chalky substance they have painted on their pots will come back to them a brilliant green or blue, after the second firing. If you have several colors to choose from, set up as many glazing stations. Describe the colors to the students and tell them that they must choose only one. Have them follow the instructions on the glaze bottles as to the number of coats. Glaze the pots inside and out. DO NOT GLAZE THE BOTTOMS. The pots must go back into the kiln. If the bottoms are glazed they will stick to the kiln shelf. As they finish, have the children put their dirty brushes into a can of water and their pots on a counter. The drips will need to be cleaned off the bottoms before firing, but this is best done after the glaze is dry. Use a damp sponge.

DOUBLE PINCH POTS

2nd-3rd Grades

clay, a ball the size of a large grapefruit for each child; extra clay in a bucket; assorted clay tools as for pinch pots; table covers

By second grade most children have enough dexterity to try a more complex pot-building project. They will begin with the familiar pinch pot, only this time it is necessary to make two. Demonstrate the entire procedure from start to finish, beginning with dividing the large ball of clay in half. Review the pinch pot method as you make one out of each half. The pots should be close to the same size and shape, but they need not match exactly.

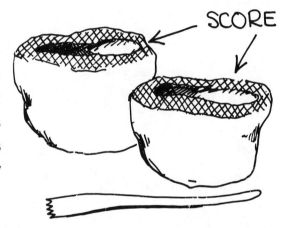

Add *scoring* to the clay vocabulary. Explain that the two pots will be joined together to make one large pot. To ensure that they won't separate as they dry, the joined edges must be roughened or scored. Do this by scraping them with a fork or clay tool.

Place one pot face down over the other one. Gently cut a hole in the top pot, a large hole for a cup or pitcher, a smaller one for a vase. Now you must "erase" the crack where the two pots have been joined. Keep fingers inside the pot for support while rubbing over the crack on the outside. Then rub the inside even though you may not be able to see what you are doing. Use your sense of touch to smooth over the joint. This is an important step! If you don't do it thoroughly, your pot may develop a crack when it dries. Gently drop the pot on the table to flatten the bottom. If the sides are fairly vertical, you can smooth them by carefully rolling the pot on the table. If you want to make a pitcher, use your index finger to drag out a spout (see diagram on the following page).

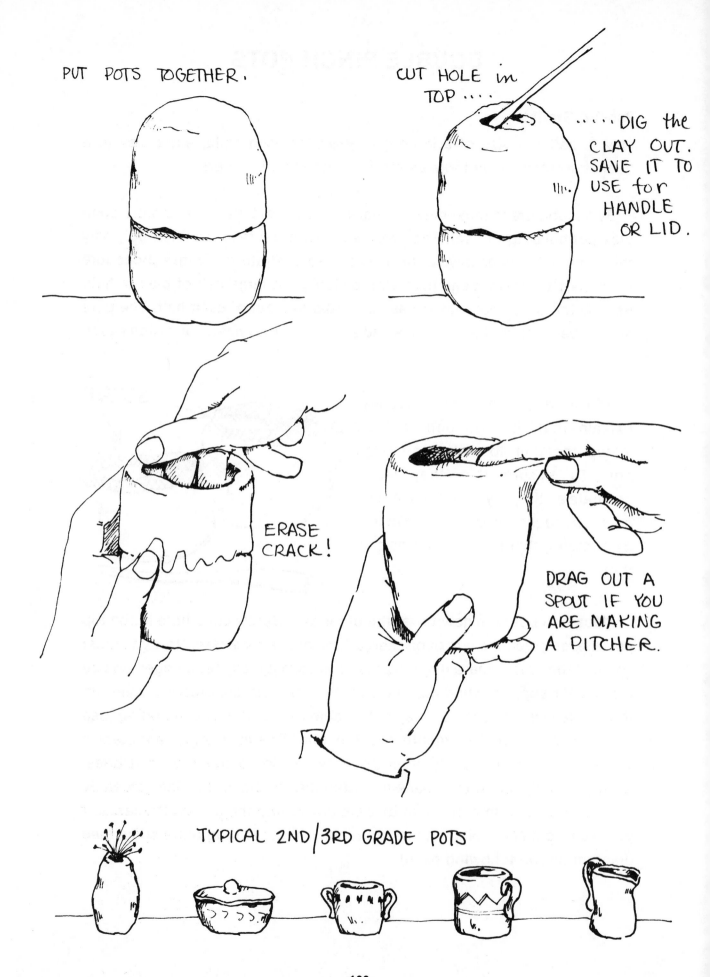

PUT POTS TOGETHER.

CUT HOLE in TOP ....

..... DIG the CLAY OUT. SAVE IT TO USE for HANDLE OR LID.

ERASE CRACK!

DRAG OUT A SPOUT IF YOU ARE MAKING A PITCHER.

TYPICAL 2ND/3RD GRADE POTS

HANDLES AND LIDS

To make a handle, roll out a worm or coil about as thick as a kindergarten pencil and longer than the height of the pot. Decide where the handle is to be joined and score the pot, top and bottom. Form the coil into a question mark, then score it where it will join. If it is too long, cut it shorter. Join and erase the cracks.

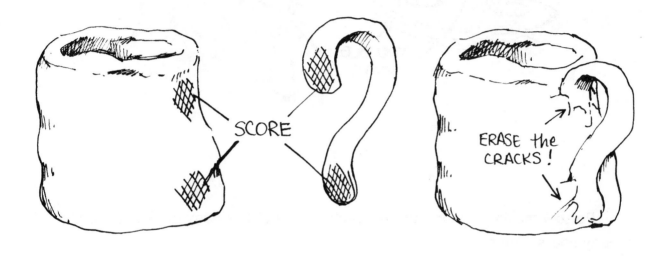

SCORE

ERASE the CRACKS!

To make a lid, begin with a ball of clay. Flatten it with your hand to a thickness of about ¼". Trim it to fit the top of the pot. Don't expect perfection here! Add a handle of your choice. Don't forget to score before attaching it to the lid. Let the lids dry beside the pots.

SCORE WHEREVER HANDLE IS TO BE ATTACHED —
SCORE HANDLE, TOO!

DON'T EXPECT A PERFECT FIT!

When the pottery is ready to be glazed, tell the children they may choose only one color for both pot and lid. Neither pot nor lid should be glazed on the bottom, but glaze should be applied to the lid's edge. Those who have handles should turn their pots upside down at some point to make sure they have gotten glaze on the inside of the handle.

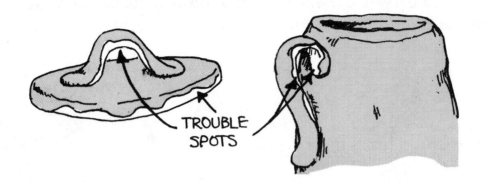

TROUBLE SPOTS

Pottery making is work for the teacher. It would be easy to skip it. Here's why you shouldn't.

1) Some children tend to be more three-dimensional in their thinking and manual dexterity. For a nondrawer, success in making a fine pot is confidence-building.

2) Clay products seem somehow more real to children than their drawings and paintings. They are certainly more permanent. The pottery will be drunk from, given to dearest relatives, used for candy dishes and sugar bowls, and treasured for years.

3) Making a pot helps a child develop a taste for what is good in pottery. Gaudy ceramic ashtrays are the only exposure many children have to pottery. This should be a clue to the teacher—no ashtrays will be allowed! You have no control over what happens after the pots go home, but you can make the children aware that pottery has many functions, the lowest of which is collecting cigarette butts.

SLAB WEED POCKET

3rd Grade

clay, a ball the size of a grapefruit for each child; clay tools (as for pinch pots); large dowels about 18″ long or rolling pins; 18″ lattice, ¼″ thick, two for each child; 9″ x 12″ burlap; table covers; paper towels; gadgets such as nuts, bolts, screws, spools, buttons, or other items to press into the clay to make a pattern or texture

Before you demonstrate, pass out the supplies EXCEPT for the rolling pins and clay. Gather the children around a table and go through the entire procedure. (To help them remember what to do, make a chart that shows each step. They can refer to it as they are working.)

Flatten the clay with your hands to a thickness of about ½″ to ¾″. Form it into an oblong or oval shape. Place the lattice on either side of the clay and roll it out until it no longer moves under the pressure of the rolling pin. Tell the students that they must always have the lattice in place when they are rolling out the clay. This ensures that it will be an even thickness throughout. Be prepared to help them with the final stages of rolling.

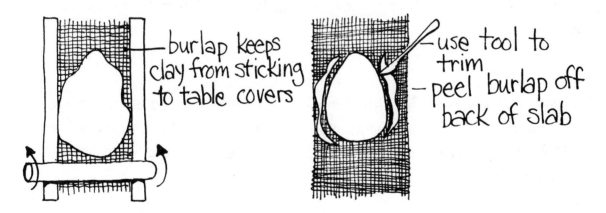

burlap keeps clay from sticking to table covers

use tool to trim
peel burlap off back of slab

Remove the lattice. Trim the clay to get rid of rough edges. The bottom of the *slab* (add that to your vocabulary list) should be wider than the top. Score along the left and right edges from the bottom to about the halfway point. To remove the slab from the burlap, turn it over on your hand and peel the burlap away from the clay. Fold up the lower half and press along the left and right sides where you have scored. Because the slab is wider at the bottom, you should have formed a pocket.

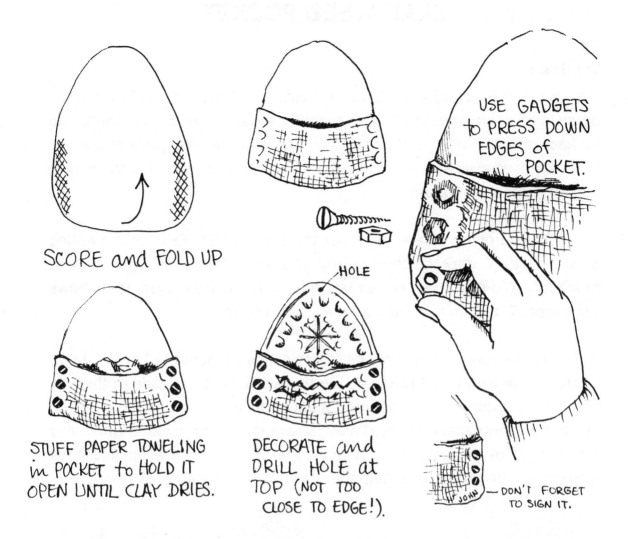

SCORE and FOLD UP

STUFF PAPER TOWELING in POCKET to HOLD IT OPEN UNTIL CLAY DRIES.

HOLE

DECORATE and DRILL HOLE at TOP (NOT TOO CLOSE TO EDGE!).

USE GADGETS to PRESS DOWN EDGES of POCKET.

JOHN — DON'T FORGET TO SIGN IT.

Wad up a paper towel—or part of one—to hold the pocket open. Decorate the upper half of the slab by making impressions in the clay with the gadgets. Finally make a hole, center top (teacher should help with this), initial the pot, and put it away to dry.

When the time comes, glaze everything but the back of the weed pocket. Redrill the hole with a pencil to make sure glaze isn't clogging it. To use the pockets, place bits of floral or oil clay inside; then insert dried flowers and weeds. Hang and enjoy!

CLAY ANIMALS

1st-2nd-3rd Grades

clay, a ball the size of a grapefruit (or an orange for younger students), one for each child; clay tools (as for pinch pots); table covers; samples of sculptures if you have any

What is sculpture? Before your students begin, they need to know the difference between two and three-dimensional art objects. Ask them if they

can give you examples of sculptures. Someone will probably think of statues in parks and museums. If you have brought a small sculpture to class, show it. It is important for the students to know that sculpture does not have a back side. Unlike pictures which hang flat against the wall, sculptures are meant to be viewed all the way around.

Demonstrate the entire procedure for making an animal. Introduce the "pinch and pull" method in which nothing is removed from the original ball of clay. Features are gently pinched and pulled out of the mass. As in painting, you should start with the large shapes first and save details (or 'de tails) for last. Begin with an oblong, potato-like shape for the animal's body.

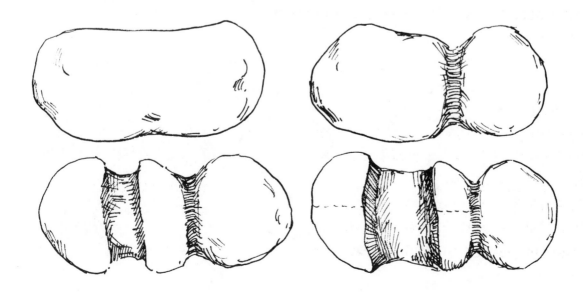

Gently squeeze out a neck or make an indentation where the head and body come together. To form the legs, turn the animal over and push your finger into the stomach, thus separating front and hind quarters. Pull the clay forward and back until you can see the division clearly. Use a tool to cut the front and back leg sections in half to form four legs. Separate the legs with

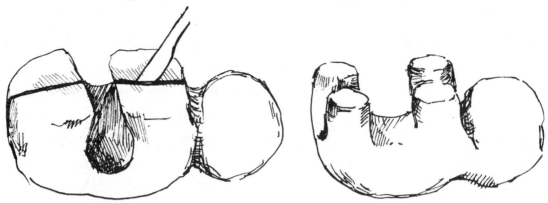

your fingers and pinch them to make them longer and rounder. Be careful not to pinch them too thin or flat. Next pinch and pull out ears, muzzles, and tails. Some students may want to wait until after the animal has been fired, then glue on a yarn tail. Talk to the kids about the positions animals get into. The clay is easy to manipulate. Show them how they can bend the legs to make the animal sit or lie down—a good idea for those who are having trouble making strong legs. A dinosaur might swing its tail and crane its neck over its shoulder. A cat could sit with one paw up as if batting at something. Action makes the animals seem more lifelike and the sculpture more interesting. If a child MUST add on clay, make sure he joins the addition securely and smooths over the crack.

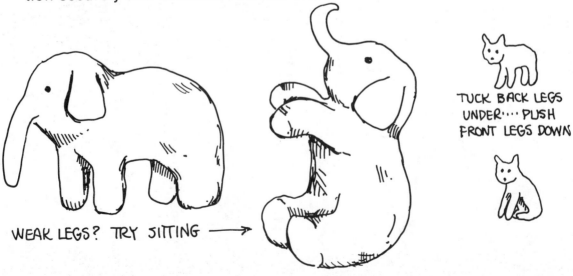

WEAK LEGS? TRY SITTING ——→

TUCK BACK LEGS UNDER···· PUSH FRONT LEGS DOWN

After the sculptures have been bisque fired, they can be painted with watercolors or tempera and finished with spray varnish or clear acrylic. Painting is preferable to glazing because painting is more immediate. If a child wants to paint spots or stripes—or blood running out of a wounded dinosaur—he can see the colors firsthand. With paint there is no mystery. What you see is what you get.

yarn tail & mane . . .

Popsicle stick can be used to cut mouth when clay is wet.

—go for a life-like pose!

If you are doing a farm, zoo, circus, or dinosaur unit, why not build a tabletop environment for the animals, complete with pens, cages, trees, and/or volcanoes? Use paper, pipe cleaners, rocks—whatever you can think of to make the place look homey. If there are any ducks, a mirror makes a good pond. Invite other classes in to see your creation.

KACHINA DOLLS

3rd Grade

clay, a grapefruit-sized ball for each child; clay tools (as for pinch pots); table covers; pictures of kachina dolls (can be found in books about Indians of the Southwest); fabric scraps; needle; thread; yarn; fake fur; small beads; feathers

The benefits from making kachina dolls are twofold. First, your students will learn about the kachina spirits and what they mean to the Indians. Secondly, they will learn to sculpt a human figure without worrying about realism. The human form is more difficult than the animal, mainly because of the number of legs. It's hard to balance a two-legged sculpture. Since kachina dolls are stylized, their legs can be short and thick.

Show the class as many pictures of kachina dolls as you can find. If you are lucky enough to own a real kachina, by all means show it to the kids. Talk or read about the meaning of the kachina. Mention that the Indians carve their dolls out of wood and that the results are rather simplified. Small details are often eliminated.

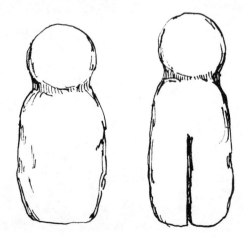

Demonstrate the method of forming a doll out of clay. Begin with a fat cylinder. Squeeze a slight ring toward the top to indicate where the head will be. Use a tool to slice through the cylinder from the bottom to the midpoint—legs. Separate the legs slightly and model them to make them

rounder. Push out at the base of the legs to make feet. Arms can be pinched and pulled out or added on. If they are added, be sure to score and erase the crack. (See Double Pinch Pots, page 101.) Pinch and pull horns, ears, and headdress shapes. Use a pencil to make holes in ears and perhaps hands.

After the dolls have been fired, they can be painted and decorated. Plan to allow at least two, thirty-minute sessions for this. Look at the kachina pictures again, this time paying attention to the surface designs. Some of the natural color of the clay can be left showing. Students should think about face and body makeup as they design with color. Finally, string beads for necklaces and earrings, make loincloths from yarn and fabric scraps, put a stick spear through the hole in the hand, add yarn or fur hair and feathers for color. These are special kachinas, because they have helped your students walk for awhile in another's moccasins.

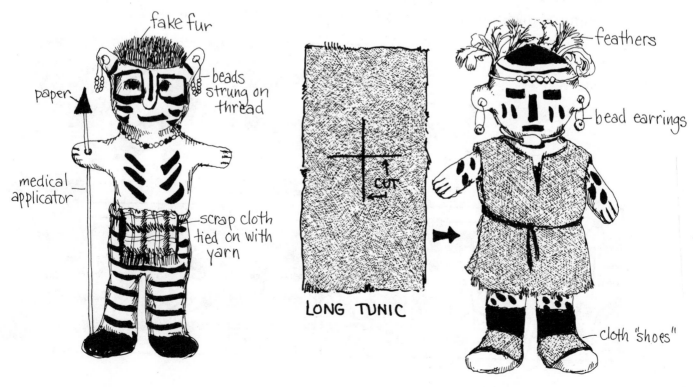

fake fur

beads strung on thread

paper

medical applicator

scrap cloth tied on with yarn

LONG TUNIC

CUT

feathers

bead earrings

cloth "shoes"

MURALS

Group projects can be satisfying experiences if properly organized and coordinated by the teacher. Mural-making helps with class spirit and gives the children a feeling of belonging. The tasks involved in making a mural fall into two main categories, the background and the subject matter.

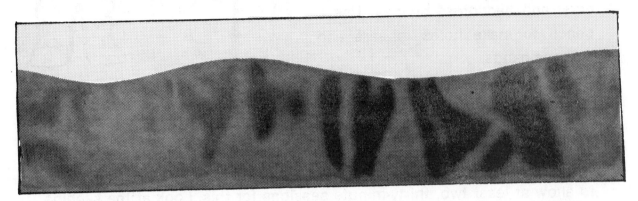

The background may be one solid color or may be more elaborate, depending on the subject matter. Fadeless paper makes good background material, because it is bright and cheery—and won't fade. If you are planning a landscape, you could lay out the background as illustrated before the children begin. If you want them to be involved in the background, have four or five children at a time paint the sky and the ground (or whatever), allowing each group about two minutes of painting time. When the time is up, the painters give their brushes to five different children. While this is going on

everybody who is not painting should be working on subject matter for the mural. You will have gotten the seat work started before the background work begins. Cut paper is a good medium for murals because the colors are bright and show up well. Pastels and oil crayons work but are a bit messy.

FOR A COLORFUL "SPRINGTIME" MURAL, KIDS MAKE CUT-PAPER FLOWERS:

center + petals + glue =

TEACHER PROVIDES BLUE SKY, TREE, BROWN BUTCHER PAPER WALL and LOTS of 3"x6" RED "BRICKS." KIDS "LAY" BRICKS BEFORE GLUING ON FLOWERS. ADD CUT-PAPER BIRDS, LEAVES, HUMPTY-DUMPTY, CLOUDS, SUN, BUTTERFLIES ·······WHATEVER!

As the children finish with their individual contributions, they should bring them to a designated location or glue them onto the background. Be sure you are there to supervise. You are part of the class, too. Although you can let the kids discuss the placement of the parts, use your own sense of design (and your authority) to make final decisions or to intervene if someone is doing something horrendous. Remind the children that larger objects should generally be placed lower and smaller objects higher on the paper. Of course, this rule wouldn't always apply, as in the case of an underwater scene.

Three mural ideas follow. Each one requires a special contribution from the teacher. The kids like having your work alongside their own. The touches that you add will make their murals extra special.

Parents, this section isn't practical for a family, unless you are ambitious or adapt the ideas for use by individuals. However, you are a rare parent if you don't find yourself involved with a group of children sometime in your career. Murals work as well with scout troops, 4-H clubs and Sunday School classes as they do with children at school.

"TEDDY BEARS' PICNIC"
For a finishing touch, outline everything with black marker.

"OUR TOWN"
Let kids who finish early make pieces of road by gluing yellow stripes to pre-cut strips of black paper.

Dark blue is added at the bottom to make the background for this mural......

"RIVERBOATS

THE SAME BACKGROUND THREE DIFFERENT WAYS

PATCHWORK QUILT

1st Grade

12″ x 12″ and 6″ x 6″ construction paper in assorted colors, markers or crayons, glue

This project begins as a lesson in pattern and design. The kids don't even need to know that they are contributing to a mural. Let each child choose one 12″ square and three 6″ squares. Tell the class to glue the smaller squares to the larger ones as you demonstrate. See illustration.

Tape a small square to the board. Have someone who is wearing plaid stand up. Ask the children if they know what that pattern is called. Tell them that plaid is simply patterns of stripes going both ways. Draw a pattern of vertical stripes on the small square, something like two skinny blue lines, one fat red, two skinny blues, one fat red, etc. Ask for a volunteer to draw the same pattern horizontally across your verticals. Ask if anyone can describe another pattern of stripes—and another, until you are sure

and so on ↓

everyone understands that there are infinite variations. Tell the children that one of their four squares must be plaid. What other kinds of patterns are there? Checks, polka-dots, florals, stripes. Almost anything can be a pattern—repetition is the key. The other three squares can be designed with patterns of each child's choice.

About mid-session have the class stop work for awhile, and ask if anyone knows what a quilt is. Talk about the reason quilts were made and how they were put together. Ask the children to pretend-sew their four squares together with black crayon (or marker) stitches.

When the children aren't around, staple their quilt squares to a bulletin board, and "stitch" them all together with black marker. For a final touch, draw and color a child's face and hands. Tear the upper half of a teddy bear out of construction paper. Add a strip of white "sheet" across the top of the quilt, and insert face, hands, and bear. Stand back and listen to the kids' reactions.

MARCHING BAND

1st-2nd Grades

white butcher paper, the length to be determined by the number of people in the band—don't cut it off the roll until you are finished gluing on the figures; 12" x 18" white drawing paper; chalkboard; chalk; oil or wax crayons; scissors; glue; a collection of rhythm band instruments; record of marching band music

This fun, noisy mural is also a figure-drawing lesson. Gather the children together on the floor and talk about parades and marching bands. Each child will draw one member of a marching band. What happens to your legs when you march? Have everybody stand. March in place slowly, observing the motion of the legs. Freeze in marching position. Notice that one leg is straight. The lifted leg comes forward and bends at the knee. Have everybody sit. Draw a

head and torso on the board. Ask a volunteer to draw the legs. Discuss the outcome of the attempt and let other kids offer suggestions. It's not unusual for the lifted leg to have extra bends. Don't insist on perfection. You are pushing the children past their schematic representations, and they are bound to have a bit of a struggle.

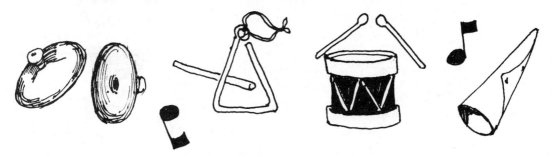

What about arms? Have children pose one at a time holding a rhythm instrument. Have them march in place, then freeze, so the rest of the class can study the position of drumming, horn blowing, flag carrying, flute playing, or cymbal crashing arms. Use a tube of rolled paper for a flute, a paper cone for a horn.

The discussion is not over yet! Prior to the class, decide on the band's colors. Make a chart (as shown), indicating the colors of pants, jackets, hats, plumes, etc. Tell the children that they have to color the uniforms on their figures according to the chart. They may complain about it, and a few will get it wrong, but help them see that a band is a unit, not a democracy! Put on the record, have everyone stand and follow you, marching, of course. March the class around the room once; then have the children drop off at their seats.

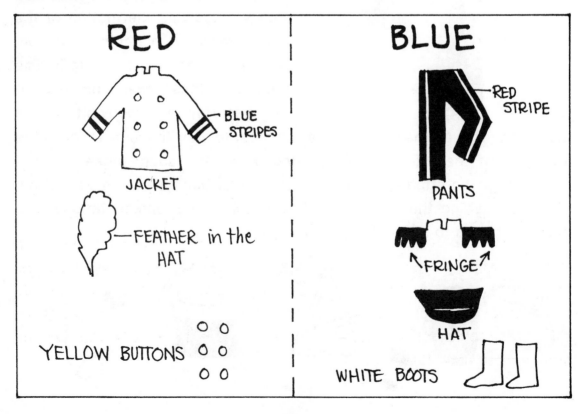

They should begin by drawing a large marching figure with chalk. Mistakes can be rubbed out with the hand or a pencil eraser, and the crayon will cover any remnants of error. Some children will need help. Try to get them going without drawing it for them. A few might be bothered by drawing a front-facing torso and side-view legs. They may work this out on their own by drawing a complete profile. Occasionally, a child will draw a complete front view with one leg much shorter, as if bent at the knee. Keep encouraging the children to show movement in the arms and legs. Have them hold an imaginary instrument and look at the position of their arms, or let them pose for each other as they are working.

When they begin to color the uniforms, ask if band colors are pale or bright. Urge everyone to push hard to get bright colors. The last step is to carefully cut the figure out. Help the kids around the difficult spots. Don't allow any sloppy cutting jobs on the mural! Supervise the gluing. If possible have a drum major, baton twirlers, or flag carrier at the head. Ask that the figures be glued one after the other without leaving gaps. Smaller ones should go up higher on the paper. The marchers will no doubt be facing all directions. No matter . . . some are just marching backwards. Leave room at the bottom to draw the center line of the street. This could be the responsibility of an early finisher.

Hang the mural when the children are not around, and have some fun yourself. Use a black marker to draw musical notes and sound effects all over the paper. If some of the figures are lost in confusion, touch them up with a black outline where needed.

Here comes the band!

CHILDREN'S GAMES

2nd-3rd Grades

sheet of black fadeless paper big enough to cover a bulletin board, 6″ x 9″ white drawing paper, black fine-point markers, pencils, crayons, scissors, glue, reproduction (or picture in a book) of Pieter Bruegel's *Children's Games*

Before the class begins, draw four or five pieces of playground equipment on the black background with white paint. See illustration.

Show the class Bruegel's painting. If you have only a small picture, gather the children around so everybody can see. Don't tell them the title. Ask them to describe what they see. When the discussion starts to lag, ask "What kind of people do the things pictured? Who plays leapfrog? Who turns somersaults? Who plays with hoops? Who wears masks?" Keep questioning until someone says, "We do!" Bruegel's painting is important, because it

shows what children did over five hundred years ago. Isn't it interesting that children are still doing some of the same things! Most kids are glad that "running the gauntlet," which is shown toward the left side, has gone out of fashion.

Have the kids take turns telling about what they do at recess. Show them the background paper, which represents the playground (blacktop). Ask the children to draw figures to add to the playground. They should draw with pencil first, then outline with marker to make the people show up better. Finally, they should color the people brightly. Urge them to use strong color. When the figures are finished, cut them out carefully and neatly. Don't leave any white paper around the edges! Help those who are having trouble cutting around small details. Have the kids think about the positions arms and legs need to be in to run, swing, hang upside down, bat, catch. As the figures are cut out, they can be glued to the background. Details such as jump ropes or chains for swings can be drawn directly on the background with a white crayon.

When all have made a contribution or two, hang the mural on the bulletin board. Ask for suggestions for a title. Vote to pick the favorite. Display Bruegel's painting near the mural. You may want to let the kids continue to add more people to their playground as they have time.